"Eye-opening research that validates parents' concerns regarding the relationship their kids have with digital technology can be found in *Digital Kids*. Dr Kutscher's easy-to-understand explanations of many topics such as multi-tasking vs multi-switching, the effects of technology on reading comprehension, and the difficulty of switching from playing video games to starting homework, makes *Digital Kids* a great resource for parents and educators!"

—*Marcella Moran, MA, LMHC,*
The Kid Organizer, thekidorganizer.com

"A comprehensive, scientifically backed, yet down-to-earth guide for parents trying to understand this confusing digital world and how it impacts their children, especially the more vulnerable. The honest, straightforward talk on parents' responsibilities for their child's internet use and how to meet them is invaluable."

—*Heidi Bernhardt, President and Executive Director,*
Centre for ADHD Awareness, Canada

"Today's children quickly gravitate to—and master—electronic devices. This leaves their parents both proud and fearful. What is the impact on social skills and brain development? The antidote to fear is knowledge, explains veteran pediatric neurologist Martin Kutscher. In this engagingly written book, he gently walks you through the issues and the ways you can create healthy balance in your child's life."

—*Gina Pera, Adult ADHD Expert, author of*
Is It You, Me, or Adult A.D.D.?

"By emphasizing social transactions and the social rules of digital society, as well as the safe use of digital media, this book will help to create boundaries and strengthen understanding of the digital world, without frightening the reader about the use and culture of social media and the internet in general. I strongly recommend this book for parents to encourage them to get involved with what their 'digital kids' are doing online."

—*Ioannis Voskopoulos, Psychologist*

by the same author

Kids in the Syndrome Mix of ADHD, LD, Autism Spectrum, Tourette's, Anxiety, and More!
The one-stop guide for parents, teachers, and other professionals
Martin L. Kutscher, MD
With contributions from Tony Attwood, PhD and Robert R. Wolff, MD
ISBN 978 1 84905 967 1
eISBN 978 0 85700 882 4

ADHD—Living without Brakes
Martin L. Kutscher, MD
ISBN 978 1 84310 873 3 (hardback)
ISBN 978 1 84905 816 2 (paperback)
eISBN 978 1 84642 769 5

Children with Seizures
A Guide for Parents, Teachers, and Other Professionals
Martin L. Kutscher, MD
ISBN 978 1 84310 823 8
eISBN 978 1 84642 490 8

DIGITAL KIDS

How to
Balance Screen Time,
and Why it Matters

Martin L. Kutscher, MD

Jessica Kingsley *Publishers*
London and Philadelphia

First published in 2017
by Jessica Kingsley Publishers
73 Collier Street
London N1 9BE, UK
and
400 Market Street, Suite 400
Philadelphia, PA 19106, USA

www.jkp.com

Library of Congress Cataloging in Publication Data
Names: Kutscher, Martin L., author.
Title: Digital kids : how to balance screen time, and why it matters / Martin L. Kutscher.
Description: London ; Philadelphia : Jessica Kingsley Publishers, 2017. | Includes bibliographical references and index.
Identifiers: LCCN 2016017094 | ISBN 9781785927126 (alk. paper)
Subjects: LCSH: Internet addiction--Popular works. | Internet addiction--Prevention. | Internet users--Mental health.
Classification: LCC RC569.5.I54 K88 2017 | DDC 616.85/84--dc23 LC record available at https://urldefense.proofpoint.com/v2/url?u=https-3A__lccn. loc.gov_2016017094&d=BQIFAg&c=euGZstcaTDllvimEN8b7jXrwqOf-v5A_CdpgnVfiiMM&r=4EemtO9R1x-uacXap7EaQ1RHPq9-MnYBwnfuC-ulpHU&m=c-2-bJeF25LtzYwasGj-HB6WlVx9wYcS4Tx9kxMpBzY&s=5_9dOnV Z1CejgaKdbihwCQuWw9DJznP5eHrwuN8WVKI&e=

British Library Cataloguing in Publication Data
A CIP catalogue record for this book is available from the British Library

ISBN 978 1 78592 712 6
eISBN 978 1 78450 296 6

Printed and bound in the United States

To our wonderful children and their loving parents,
who are learning together
how to balance the digital world

DISCLAIMER

This information is for educational purposes only, and does not constitute medical advice. Information and recommendations on this topic are subject to change. Cited references do not necessarily represent the views or the endorsement of the author.

CONTENTS

Introduction. **11**

The recent explosion of digital technology
and services.   12

The Internet: The good part.   12

The extent of screen-time usage   13

Haven't people declared the "end of civilization"
with previous advances?   14

The parents' dilemma and role in setting limits   16

The problems of screen-time use are on a spectrum . .   16

Organization of this book.   17

1. Problems with the *Use* of Digital Technology **19**

Psychological/learning effects of digital technology .   19

Does technology interfere with classroom work?.   20

Does taking notes on a laptop (rather than with a pen and paper)
interfere with learning?.   22

Does reading on a screen interfere with in-depth learning? . .   23

How does our attention system work?   28

"But Mom, it's so boring when I'm not playing video games":
The need for down-time   33

Screens interfere with developing voluntary attention   34

Areas where digital learning does excel   35

Summary of digital vs. print effects on learning   36

Other psychological effects of digital technology   37

Association with other psychological conditions   39

Neurological effects of digital technology abuse. . . .   40

Physical effects of digital media use   42

2. Problems with the *Content* of Digital Technology 45

Social media 46
   The appeal of social media 47
   Cyber-bullying 48
   Sexting 49
   Giving out too much information 50
   Hiding too much information 51
   The good part of social media 52

Does exposure to pornography and other media affect
sexuality? 52
   Teenage sexuality in the US 53
   Teenage exposure to sexual content in US media 54
   The relationship between media exposure and adolescent
     sexual behavior 54

Does media exposure increase the risk of violent
behavior? 55

Do violent video games lead to violent behavior? . . . 57

Does media affect substance use? 58

Resultant American Academy of Pediatrics
recommendations regarding digital media 58

3. Problems Regarding Specific Populations 61

Very young children and screen time 62
   Statistics on usage 62
   Is there any benefit to screen time for children less than
     2 years old? 63
   What about 3–5-year-olds? 64
   Does "background" or "second-hand" TV interfere with child
     development? 64
   Am I really harming my infant if they have occasional
     screen time? 65

Children with ADHD and screen time 66
   ADHD traits that make screen time so appealing 66
   The risk of ADHD and excessive Internet/gaming use 67

Children with ASD and screen time 69
   ASD traits that make screen time so appealing 69

4. The Parental Role 75

What kind of role model am I for my child? 75

How do I set limits for my child? 79
   Use technology to help limit technology 79
   Help the child develop voluntary attention control 80
   Set explicit time rules in advance 82

All pigs are created equal, but some pigs are ready for
more equality than others. 85
Another adult responsibility: Teach how to evaluate
information on the web. 86

5. **Setting Up the Rules: The Family Meeting and Agreement** **89**

The family meeting 89
Considerations before the family meeting 89
The agreement. 91

6. **Internet Addiction: The Far End of Internet Problems**
(with Natalie Rosin) **95**

Internet problems cover a whole range of severity. . . **95**
What is an addiction? **96**
How does someone get addicted? **99**
The psychological basis of addiction. 99
The biological basis of addiction. 99
How common is Internet addiction? **100**
Why is digital media so addictive?. **100**
Ready access. 101
Digital technology is fascinating. 102
Digital technology meets psychological needs, especially those
of teens. 102
What are particularly addictive Internet activities? . . **103**
What personal traits are associated with Internet
addiction?. **104**
How do we treat Internet addiction? **105**
The basics 105
Interventions with a therapist 106

7. **Summary** **109**

The recent explosion of digital technology
and services **109**
The extent of screen-time usage **110**
The parents' dilemma and role in setting limits **111**
Problems with the use of digital technology. **111**
Does technology interfere with classroom work?. 111
Which is better? Taking notes with a pen and paper or with
a laptop? 112
Does reading on a screen interfere with in-depth learning? . . 112
How does our attention system work? 113
Areas where digital learning does excel 116

Other psychological effects of the Internet   117
Association with other psychological conditions   117
Neurological effects of Internet abuse   117
Physical effects of digital media use   118
Problems with the content of digital technology . . .   118
Social media issues.   118
Does exposure to pornography and other media affect
   sexuality?.   118
Does media exposure increase the risk of violent behavior? . .   119
Do violent video games lead to violent behavior?   119
Does media affect substance use?.   120
Resultant American Academy of Pediatrics recommendations
   regarding digital media   120
Problems regarding specific populations.   121
Very young children and screen time.   121
Children with ADHD and screen time   122
Children with ASD and screen time   123
The parental role   124
What kind of role model am I for my child?   124
How do I set limits for my child (until they are mature
   enough to limit themselves)?   124
**Setting up the rules: The family meeting and
agreement. 125**
The family meeting   125
Internet addiction: The far end of Internet problems .   125
What is an addiction?   125
The psychological basis of addiction   126
What are particularly addictive Internet activities?   126
How do we treat Internet addiction?.   127
Interventions with a therapist   127

References   128

Resources   132

About the Authors   136

Index   137

INTRODUCTION

Everyone is in their own corner, glued to their screen! I feel like I'm herding cats! I just want everyone to put down their devices and talk to each other over dinner.

My five-year-old is constantly begging to use my smartphone. My teenage daughter never puts her cell away. It is always in her hand or a few inches away on the table. At work, the hallways and elevators are filled with people checking their email or texts.

I'm worried about my children's technology use. Why does my son scream when I try to get him off the computer? Is my daughter honest about her Internet activities? Just how much screen time is too much? Just how do I set limits without starting World War III? What effect is all of this media and technology having on my children's brains, learning and behavior?

As a pediatric behavioral neurologist, I hear a constant litany of concerns from parents about their children's—and their own—often unending attraction to digital technology. As we shall see, these concerns are not unfounded, nor are they insurmountable. The antidote to fear is knowledge, and this book will provide you with the knowledge you need to successfully confront the issues. We need facts in order to motivate ourselves and our children to balance our behavior. I'll explain *why* this balance matters, by exploring the effects of extensive screen use on our brains and our lives. I'll also discuss *how* to balance screen time in order to successfully co-exist with the plethora of benefits and threats coming to our digital kids.

The recent explosion of digital technology and services

The rapid explosion of technology in the past 15 years has led to unprecedented opportunities and challenges for us all. Just consider the new technological *devices* since 2000: iPods, iPhones, iPads, Android, camera phones, broadband Internet modems, Wi-Fi, HD TVs, and Roku. New technology *services* since 2000 include Facebook, Twitter, Skype, Instagram, MySpace, LinkedIn, iTunes, Netflix, Hulu, YouTube, hi-tech online games, Apps, and Firefox (Rosen 2012). That's all on top of our "old" technology, such as video games, texting, email, and television. Collectively referred to as "screen time," these activities have been quite a lot to adjust to in just a few decades, especially for our human brains, which evolved on the savannah over the millennia to handle a quite different and slower-paced set of stimuli.

Note that since the Internet is one type of digital technology, and that most digital information involves a screen, I will be using the terms *digital technology, Internet,* and *screen time* mostly interchangeably.

The Internet: The good part

There are a lot of good things to say about the Internet and digital technology. It allows for a virtually limitless proliferation of news, intellectual thought, art, entertainment, and other information. It allows for the learning of new skills. It is an outlet for creativity, and for a range of opinions. It allows for unprecedented connectivity of people with similar interests and goals. It allows for instant communication with fellow workers, friends, loved ones, and strangers around the globe. It allows for myriad minds to work together on solving a problem. Plus, it's a lot of fun, and aren't we allowed to have some of that in our lives? We can go on forever. All of this is delivered to our room 24/7, 365 days/year if we wish.

Of course, for each potential positive aspect of digital technology, a negative concern can be raised. Since the good parts of digital technology are so readily observable, I'll be focusing on the often unrecognized, more worrisome parts.

The extent of screen-time usage

This technology takes up a tremendous amount of our children's day (and night). According to the American Academy of Pediatrics (2013) policy statement:

- 8–10-year-old children spend nearly 8 hours/day on media.

- Older children and teens spend more than 11 hours/day on media.

- 71% of children have a TV or Internet device in their room.

- 3 out of 4 young people aged 12–17 have a cell phone.

- 1 in 3 teens sends more than 100 texts/day (largely replacing phone use).

- Our children spend more time with media than in school, and media use is second only to sleep as the leading activity.

- 2 out of 3 children and teens say that their parents have no media rules.

(AAP 2013)

Here are a few more statistics:

- Teens received and sent 3705 texts/month—about 6/hour (Rosen 2012).

- 62% of iGeneration (teenage) students check their digital devices more frequently than every 15 minutes (Rosen 2012).

- Facebook had 1.19 billion users in 2013, 50% of whom logged in daily (Griffiths, Kuss and Demetrovics 2014).

- It is not just children who are so hooked on their screens: 1 in 3 adults says that they check their mobile device before getting out of bed in the morning (Rosen 2012).

What are the 8–18-year-olds actually doing during their recreational computer time (not including school work, TV, or music)?

- 25% social networking

- 19% playing games

- 6% on video sites

- 12% on other websites

- 13% instant messaging

- 6% checking email

- 5% looking at graphics/photos

- 5% other.

(Rideout 2010)

We'll have plenty of other statistics to ponder as we proceed through the book.

Haven't people declared the "end of civilization" with previous advances?

Are we over-reacting? With the invention of writing several thousand years ago, prominent philosophers predicted the end of anyone mastering anything in depth—given that no one would have to remember anything once it was written down. Five hundred years ago, it was thought that the Gutenberg printing press would bring about an avalanche of "junk" via unscreened mass production, rather than written information filtering through the bottleneck of scribes. Books would be everywhere! Heaven help us! Does all this sound familiar as we discuss the Internet? Indeed, throughout history, the fearful specter of information overload has been raised by each new innovation in communication. Yet the current explosion of available information does differ in several ways from the previous revolutions.

First, these days there really is way, way too much information for anyone to remember. We need to be able to sift through all the junk and off-load some of this material from our own brain to a place where the facts can be easily verified. One long-established means of doing this has been to store information in other people's brains—for example, doctors, lawyers, accountants, teachers, plumbers, and electricians—but even these specialists need to off-load their ever-evolving fund of knowledge. Another method is to transfer information to the Internet, and query it with Google. It is possible that relinquishing technical information frees up the brain, allowing it to learn new information, while retaining access to previous knowledge when needed.

Second, this current method of communicating information also allows us to interact with each other in real time. We are forming new kinds of human interactions both at work/school and at home through email or tidbits of text rather than face-to-face or telephone speech. This is an experiment in human relationships that is being carried out in real life.

Third, digital communication now allows the propagation of visual and sound information. Thus the Internet affects not only writing but also our "free-time" entertainment. In other words, the advancement of the Internet affects not just what we read (and how we read it) but how we relate to each other and entertain ourselves. In short, it affects just about everything.

The parents' dilemma and role in setting limits

Parents watch their digital kids spending hours on their digital devices, and are torn between the emotions of *pride* over their prodigy's technical prowess, *happiness* that they are preparing their child for the future, and *fear* about the as yet unknown possible effects of all of this technology use on their child's brain, social skills and future. What's the proper balance?

Technology by itself is neither good nor bad. Rather, as we shall see, the uses and limits of technology (which we should be teaching our children) are what determine whether it has a good or bad effect on society. It is not our children's fault if we, their parents and teachers, have failed to teach them how to balance screen-time use. But, then again, we are the first generation to have to teach this stuff, and we don't have any role models from past generations to guide us.

The problems of screen-time use are on a spectrum

Screen-time problems run along a spectrum of severity. At the mildest end are the problems we perceive among typical, well-functioning children/teens, such as texting multiple times in an hour or failing to check the reliability of Internet sources before quoting them. Then there are the kids whose screen-time activities result in modest family discord and inefficient work, but who are still able to lead a balanced life with decent grades, a good set of friends, and participation in other activities such as sports. At the most severe end, there are those who suffer from what can be called a true Internet addiction: an inability to control one's digital/Internet behavior despite significant resultant problems (e.g., falling grades, withdrawal from friends and activities, or significant family turmoil). The degree of resistance that you meet when trying to get your child off their device provides a good clue as to their degree of screen dependence. People with a high degree of dependence may react vociferously as a withdrawal symptom when a parent tries to limit access to screen time. The extreme end of the spectrum of problematic screen time (i.e., Internet addiction) is the subject of Chapter 6.

The concept of a spectrum of problems is not unique to issues with screen time; it is actually applied to a whole host of neurobehavioral disorders. Extensive studies of children find a spectrum of difficulties in the areas of autism, Attention Deficit Hyperactivity Disorder (ADHD), anxiety, depression, and psychosis (White 2015). In fact, the American Psychiatric Association (APA 2013) has discarded previous attempts to carve out specific syndromes among children with autistic features, and renamed the whole range as "Autism Spectrum Disorder" (ASD). It is indeed possible to have "a touch" of conditions such as depression, dyslexia, or problematic screen time.

Just like children with "a touch" of anxiety, children with "a touch" of screen-time problems may never be brought to clinical attention. That is a shame, because there is much reason to believe that early prevention and treatment can improve the outcome of children with sub-clinical problems.

Organization of this book

There is a lot of material that I'll try to present in a comprehensive way. In order to be useful, though, it needs to be read—and keeping the text brief helps hectic families achieve that goal. For each issue raised, I'll present statistical data (so that you can judge the extent of the problem) and a sampling of the research done on the issue, followed by a summary statement on the topic. I'll also try to avoid an overwhelming number of prevention and treatment suggestions, focusing rather on select, high-yield interventions.

A glance at the table of contents reveals the following structure to this book: Chapters 1 to 3 focus mostly on why striking a balance between the digital and real worlds is important, and Chapters 4 and 5 focus primarily on how to achieve that balance.

Chapter 1: Problems posed by the actual use of digital technology as the conduit through which information flows, as distinct from the specific information flowing through that conduit. I will focus on a range of problems, such as shallow reading, constant interruptions interfering with our work, and lack of down-time during which to think creatively. I'll cover screen time's effects from a psychological/learning perspective, a neurological perspective, and even a physical health perspective.

Chapter 2: Problems posed by the content of digital technology. The focus will include social media, bullying, sexting, pornography, violence, lyrics, and more.

Chapter 3: Problems associated with specific populations. I'll look at young age, ADHD, and the autism spectrum.

Chapter 4: The parental role. I'll be discussing treatment recommendations as we work through the chapters, but this chapter will focus entirely on the role of parents as role models, guides, and limit-setters.

Chapter 5: The family meeting and agreement section will focus on verbal discussion leading to a signed agreement regarding an appropriate balance of digital media use and limits.

Chapter 6: The problem of Internet addiction. We will discuss causes, prevention, and treatments of this increasingly common problem.

Chapter 7: Summary. Here I sum up the preceding material. This chapter can serve as a review but is also comprehensive enough to be a standalone text for people who just want to read the highlights from the book.

As parents, teachers, and children, we all try to learn from each other, so keep in mind that it's nobody's fault, but it's everyone's problem. Good luck to us all!

Chapter 1

PROBLEMS WITH THE *USE* OF DIGITAL TECHNOLOGY

In this chapter we'll focus on the problems associated with the use of digital technology as a *conduit* (in contrast to the problems caused by the *content* coming through that conduit). We will start with psychological/learning effects, then address neurological effects, and then effects on physical health.

Psychological/learning effects of digital technology

The term "digital natives" has been applied to people who have grown up with digital technology, in contrast to "digital immigrants," who have adopted the technology later in their life. To summarize, digital natives:

> gravitate towards a "shallow" mode of information processing characterized by rapid attention shifting and reduced deliberations. Relative to older generations, they engage in increased multi-tasking behaviors that are linked to increased distractibility and poor executive control abilities. (Loh 2015, p.2)

Let's look at some of the studies leading to those conclusions. According to one teacher survey regarding the problem with technology in schools:

- Nearly 90% of teachers felt that technology has created a distracted generation with short attention spans.

- 60% felt it hindered writing and face-to-face communication i.e., communication with full sentences and longer has lost out to short snippets in writing or media.

- Almost 50% felt it hurt critical thinking and homework ability.

- 76% felt students were conditioned to find quick answers.

(Porter 2013)

In short, technology is changing the way our students learn, and not always for the better.

Does technology interfere with classroom work?

Yes. According to a student survey (Rosen 2012), 62% of the iGeneration (teens) check for text messages and 32% check into Facebook every 15 minutes or less, although the survey did not specify if that frequency changed during class. In contrast, only 18% of baby boomers check for text messages and 8% check into Facebook every 15 minutes or less.

In another survey (Baron 2015), university students were asked how often they used their cell phones while in class for non-class-related reasons. The average college student reported such use 11 times daily, while 15% of students used their cell more than 30 times during class. Estimating 3 hours of class per day, the latter amounts to more than 10 times per class period!

All of this activity comes at a price in learning. In one study, students who sent text messages while watching a lecture had exam scores 19% below those of the students who did not text (Thompson 2014).

When students were asked about texting during class time, the following percentages agreed or strongly agreed:

- 77% felt that *receiving* text messages hurt their ability to learn during a lecture.

- 72% felt that *sending* text messages hurt their ability to learn during a lecture.

- 37% felt that they got distracted when *someone else received* a text during class.

- 31% felt that they got distracted when *someone else sent* a text during class.

- 49% of them still felt it was okay to text during class.

(Rosen 2012)

Thus, students recognized that texting in school not only interfered with their own learning, but also interfered with other students' attention; however, nearly half of them felt it was okay to do so.

Not surprisingly, allowing web access (i.e., not just texting access) to students during a lecture didn't fare well, either. One group of students was allowed to surf the web during class, while a second group kept their laptops closed. Students in the first group did indeed look at lecture-related sites, but some also went shopping, watched videos and caught up on email. Even those students who only surfed for relevant topics recalled significantly less of the lecture's content than those who kept their laptop closed (Carr 2011).

Many studies reveal that the majority of students say they use their electronic devices during class to text, browse, or consume media. The results of these studies agree with my own informal survey of patients, who, when asked, almost all say that students in their classes are using classroom laptops/ iPads for non-educational activities. Even those who have monitored or limited Internet access still use their laptops for offline gaming. If an adult approaches, they simply hit a button that switches the screen to a legitimate activity. The CD (remember those?) version of *MAD* magazine even contains a "panic button," which, if pressed when an adult checks in, pulls up a Word document that reads something to the effect of

"I can't believe my parents fell for this again." School systems that are switching to all-digital experiences for their students must ask themselves if the advantages are worth the distractions.

Does taking notes on a laptop (rather than with a pen and paper) interfere with learning?

Yes, probably. There are many apparent reasons for the superiority of pen and paper for learning. There are the benefits that come from the actual formation of the letters by the student's hand and from the need to synthesize the lecture material into their own words—handwriting is relatively slow and so eliminates the possibility of taking verbatim notes. Also, keyboards are attached to computers with their multitude of distractions, and it is harder to navigate around the page to add in additional pieces of information while simultaneously trying to listen to the teacher. First, let's look at two issues in more detail.

One study of the benefit of writing by hand was done in the context of spelling. Students were assigned to learn the spelling of 30 words using one of three practice methods: (1) using a pencil to write out the words, (2) using letter tiles to spell out the words, or (3) typing the words on a keyboard. Students who practiced using handwriting did best on a subsequent spelling test (Duran and Frederick 2016). In other studies, people reproducing letters from novel alphabets using handwriting showed better ability in orientating the characters correctly than those who practiced by typing the characters. The authors contended that hand movements during writing helped to consolidate character recognition and orientation—skills also needed in reading (Duran and Frederick 2016).

Now, we turn to the subject of which way—by hand or by keyboard—students can take the most effective notes. A study by Mueller and Oppenheimer (2014) of 65 college students at Princeton and UCLA showed that those who used laptops (disconnected from the Internet) were able to take more notes than those who took notes with a pen. However, although both groups did equally well on a test of *facts* given during the presentation, the students who used a laptop did less well on tests that contained *conceptual* questions that required synthesis of the material. The authors hypothesized that the high speed of typing led to a relatively passive and mindless verbatim transcription. In contrast, in order to keep up, those students who took notes by hand had to distill the lecture down to just the crux of the material, thereby engaging with it actively during class. In a follow-up part of the study, this advantage of handwriting persisted even after the students were advised to slow down while taking notes.

Although there is some variation in the findings, current studies suggest caution in switching to keyboards for note-taking. New technologies and the strategies of future students may change the recommendations.

Does reading on a screen interfere with in-depth learning?

Yes. Let's examine four reasons for this:

1. Screens lack a tactile experience.

2. Hypertext is distracting and hard to navigate.

3. Shallow reading becomes the norm.

4. Digital distractions are right there on the machine.

Reading on a screen lacks a tactile experience

Reading is a multi-sensory experience. According to research, the brain's act of reading uses not just sight but touch. There is something about holding a physical page of material that makes it more absorbable: "The shift from paper to screen doesn't just change the way we navigate a piece of writing. It also influences the degree of attention we devote to it and the depth of our immersion in it" (Carr 2011, p.90).

Reading on a screen makes it harder to navigate and orient oneself, especially with hypertext

Hypertext (clickable web links) is one of the web's most important tools. Indeed, hypertext is the reason why the web is called "the web." The user jumps from one spot to another with the click of the mouse, and then to another, and then to another—forming a web of jumps. Often, exactly where you are and how you got there may not be exactly clear. That's fine if you are just trying to continually refine your search for specific information.

However, hypertext seems to be a major detractor when you are attempting to read a longer, cohesive text: "Research continues to show that people who read linear text comprehend more, remember more, and learn more than those who read text peppered with links" (Carr 2011, p.127). To give just one of many research examples, 35 adults were given a short story to read in the usual linear text format, and were compared to another 35 adults who were given the same story to read in a version with hypertexts such as would be found on a web page. Even though the hypertext readers took longer, 3 out of 4 reported problems following the text, compared to 1 in 10 readers who were given the linear text.

How can it be that hypertext diminishes comprehension? There seem to be two reasons. First, there is the visual distraction of the blue text. More importantly, though, at each hypertext the reader's brain has to stop what it was doing (understanding the line of reasoning of the author) and instead devote mental processing to the question, "Should I take this hypertext jump or not?" It doesn't seem like that big a deal, but it is enough to bring the logic of the story to a screeching halt. After all, it is an important decision: who knows what content is behind that link? It is like a game show: Who knows what prize is behind door number one?! By the time the brain has figured out what decision to make about the hyperlink, it may have forgotten what it was previously thinking about. After all, the brain is limited in how many things it can keep in mind/work on simultaneously (a skill called "working memory," the brain's scratchpad). There are only so many neurons to go around.

In addition to hypertext, there is another feature of reading on the screen that makes it harder to find where you are while reading. Given a screen's ability to scroll, to alter the size of the text, to alter how many columns it presents, etc. (i.e., to continually change what the reader sees), it is hard to form a reliable visualization of the material. You can't just say to yourself, "It was at the bottom of the left side of the page towards the back of the book," because the next time you access the material, it may not be in the same spot visually. Long articles are not broken down into pages, further confounding the reader's sense of where they are in the piece. All of this matters because "a good spatial mental representation of the physical layout of the text leads to better reading comprehension" (Greenfield 2015, p.215). The miniature screen on a smartphone only compounds the problem. Many people find it easier to flip through the pages of a book or printout than to re-locate the spot on a screen.

These negative effects of hypertext reading are not inevitable, though. Using a navigational support structure may be helpful. Certain reader characteristics, such as the ability to see the "big picture," prior knowledge of the subject, and increased interest in the subject all help to mitigate the confusion (Loh 2015).

Digital technology may lead to shallower comprehension

In addition to being problematic because it confuses the reader as to where they are actually reading, hypertext jumps are also a major cause of shallow reading. In traditional printed books, the author has (presumably) spent considerable time devising a logical story or line of reasoning. As the reader works their way through the book, they can stop and ponder about the unfolding material. When they have finished thinking about what they just read, the book is still there—ready to lead the reader again along a lengthy, fully thought-out trail of logic. Hypertext spells the death of an author-driven line of reasoning. <u>Click here for more information.</u> They take you all over, from place to place, from author to author, from subject to subject—and rarely return you to your jumping-off point of that well-thought-out, comprehensive text that you started out with. Instead, the viewer finds themselves skimming sites (i.e., shallow reading) as they jump around looking for the next quick rewarding tidbit. Indeed, the average web page holds the reader for 18 seconds. Essential as it is, the ability to skim for relevant information should not be the only reading skill that we teach children. (By the way, did you find yourself distracted by the above mock hyperlink, and whether to try clicking on it? Of course you can't. This is a print book. However, if you had forgotten what we were just discussing, this little experiment shows the power of losing one's place from distracting digressions, such as jumping along hypertext.)

Search engines are part of the problem as well. Don't get me wrong, I love Google. I couldn't function any more without it…or PubMed for my medical research…or Amazon's search features. It's just that they take us right to the direct hit, which for many of us is all we read. This, again, avoids the surrounding logic intended by the author, and we may also miss the context of that direct search hit. A review of university student reference citations in their research papers showed that 46% were to the first page of the source, and 77% were to the first three pages—college students doing research almost never get past the first three pages (Baron 2015)! This is yet another source of potential shallow reading.

After conducting a survey of the research habits of 400 Canadian students, the study authors concluded that students felt that online materials were fine for picking up specific elements of materials, but that for engaging in substantial work, print books were preferred. Print gave a sense of the whole (Baron 2015).

There is concern that the reliance upon shallow reading may interfere with the development of deep reading skills such as thoughtful pondering, critical analysis and inferential thinking. It is feared that neurological connections required for deep reading, such as brain areas involved in visual processing and phonological processing, may not be generated in those people who learn primarily via shallow reading (Loh 2015).

Reading on a digital device is distracting

Reading on an Internet-enabled device or one with pre-loaded video games is highly distracting. 90% of students felt that they were more likely to be multi-tasking while reading digitally, while only 1% felt that a hard copy would make them more likely to multi-task. 9% felt that the medium (electronic or paper) didn't matter when it came to multi-tasking.

And, let's not forget all of those ads vying for our attention, and pulling us away from the author's purpose. So far, no one has figured out how to put a pop-up ad in a print book, but the ads on the Internet keep getting more invasive. They seem to pop up on the website even if you have pop-ups blocked on your settings. Many of the ads use movement, which immediately grabs your attention, because animal brains have powerful movement detectors. (Nearby movement means that you are about to get your own or become another creature's lunch. As such, movement forcefully snatches our attention. This is also part of the reason why video games and videos engage our attention so well.)

Of course, we could always ask our students to turn off their Internet connection while trying to work. Yeah, like that's going to happen.

Readers clearly *prefer* hard copy reading (even if it isn't a better learning tool)

Although there is plenty of evidence that digital reading, especially online, interferes with learning, the evidence is still somewhat inconclusive. It is pretty conclusive, though, that readers *prefer* reading on hard copy vs. via digital screen by 89% vs. 11%, and will choose a hard copy over a digital version if given the choice. The numbers are fairly constant, whether surveying US, Japanese, or German students.

It appears that the length of the material plays a role in preference. Students didn't care which medium was used when engaging with short texts such as newspaper articles. However, 92% of US students preferred hard copy for long texts in school work and reading for pleasure. Students preferred the experience of feeling the pages, knowing their place in the text, the ability to flip back and forth, and even the smell of the book. They liked the idea of personalizing their possession with handwritten notes. They appreciated less eyestrain (Baron 2015). They also appreciated not being distracted by all the things that their digital device could take them to with a click of a button.

Neuroscientist Baron concludes, "Given these findings, I can only wonder why the educational establishment is pushing students toward digital reading" (Baron 2015, p.181).

How does our attention system work?

Before moving on, we need to lay some groundwork knowledge about how our attention system works. You'll see the point of all of this in just a few minutes.

There are overlapping explanations of how we control our attention; or, perhaps, how our attention controls us (Levitin 2014; Palladino 2015). Let's see if we can put them all together and use that basic knowledge to see how digital technology affects our ability to generate down-time, to multi-task, and to train our volitional control of where we focus our conscious attention.

There are basically three types of attentional networks continually jockeying with each other for expression:

- *Stay-on-task network.* This requires willful attention to a given job. It is the function that allows us to actually execute a plan in a linear fashion. For example, writing an essay requires sustained, deliberate concentration moving from analysis of the topic, to organizing thoughts, to writing the essay, to handing it in. The stay-on-task network is the "Do it!" network.

The stay-on-task network is also called "voluntary attention." It originates with self-directed, voluntary effort. As such, it is harder to maintain. It can also be considered "top-down" attention, referring to the anatomic location of voluntary attention centers being evolutionarily placed in the "top" part of the brain— attempting to exert their control over lower parts of the brain that are concerned with our basic animal instincts.

- *Sensory/emergency network.* No matter what else we are doing, our sensory network is constantly scanning our environment for issues of safety or opportunity. Like a news bulletin, it breaks through any state of mind. We have already seen how our motion detectors are constantly at work, but we constantly scan our environment with other senses too. These sensory detectors also pull us into multi-media and colorful moving video games. Once the stimulus has been detected, the stay-on-task network becomes engaged to deal with the situation. For example, even while asleep, a parent's sound detectors alert them to the sound of a crying baby. Once the sensory/emergency network has alerted the parent, the stay-on-task network decides that hunger is the problem and keeps the parent focused on feeding the infant.

  The sensory/emergency network is a type of "involuntary attention." Importantly, it requires no willful intent from the person. As a matter of safety, it is always switched on and is activated automatically. It is passive, and originates with stimuli, not willful effort.

- *Daydreaming network.* This comes into play when the other networks are not actively dealing with a situation.

It is the time when the brain ponders, thinks in a creative non-linear fashion, consolidates learning, and restores itself. It occurs during down-time, sleep, and even during reading when we pause to consider the significance of what we just read. The daydreaming network is given its space when there is nothing else to do. *It's not only okay to be bored; some boredom is essential for the brain to function well.* The daydreaming network is another type of involuntary attention, as the brain is free to float wherever it pleases.

You may have been wondering, "How does the brain switch between networks?" Actually, you probably weren't wondering that, but it is important to deal with it, anyway. A part of the brain called the insula is believed to be involved in the switch (Levitin 2014). This act of switching takes energy, and can be fatiguing and stressful. "Many studies have shown that switching between just two tasks can add to our cognitive load, impeding our thinking and increasing the likelihood that we'll overlook or misinterpret important information" (Carr 2011, p.133).

Why is all of this important? First, it is part of the answer to the question, "Why can my child pay attention to video games, but not to his homework?" Answer: The strategic, stay-on-task part of attention in video games is constantly bolstered by the sensory/emergency network, which is involuntary, continuous, and effortless. Writing an essay with paper and pencil does not have this effortless sensory draw, and instead relies primarily on voluntary and fatiguing effort. The more your child complains about a task or avoids it, the more likely it is that the voluntary network is being more heavily challenged. Notice that voluntary and involuntary attention often work together to varying degrees.

An understanding of attentional systems is also important because it lays the framework for understanding two other screen-time issues: temptation to multi-task, and lack of down-time.

"But Mom, I can pay attention to more than one thing at a time!" The myth of "multi-tasking"

How does our attention system deal with "multi-tasking"?

It doesn't. There's no such thing as "multi-tasking." Rather, current thinking is that people "multi-switch" back and forth so frequently from one activity to another that they get the sensation that they are doing two things simultaneously, but actually they are only paying attention to one thing at any given moment. You can't type a text message and read your textbook at the same time!

So, let's re-word the question: How does our attention system deal with "multi-*switching*"?

Not so great. In one of many studies, participants had a computer and a television in the same environment. They were not told to "multi-task," yet they were observed to switch between the two on average four times per minute—a total of 120 times over the half-hour observation (Loh 2015). They may have thought they were "multi-tasking," but they were actually multi-switching. In another study, students were asked to study for 15 minutes in a familiar environment. Participants were observed to actually be studying for only 10 minutes, with the amount of switching to another task being correlated to the amount of technology available. Another study showed that even being seated within sight of others who were "multi-tasking" on their computers interfered with recall of material being learned. All of this is perhaps a warning to those of us who like to work with the TV on in the background, or with digital technology readily available while trying to work.

Although most of us think we can multi-switch efficiently, only certain tasks go well together. "Multi-tasking" with music is the easiest for people of all ages. In fact, there is reason to believe that music may actually promote learning for some people. Certainly, listening to music may be less distracting than listening to your siblings argue with each other, or the clanging of pots and pans—functioning as a type of white noise. (Difficulty might arise from using a smartphone to play the music, which opens up a whole range of distractions during homework time. A radio might be better, or dig out an old digital music player that doesn't have Internet or video capabilities.) Baby boomers, who reported the most trouble "multi-tasking," also found that watching TV and eating seemed possible to do along with other tasks. All ages surveyed found it hardest to "multi-task" when texting, reading books, and playing video games (Rosen 2015).

People who keep their Internet/smartphone on and are available to interruptions are frequently distracted. Observations of computer programmers found them to be interrupted every 3 minutes. Laptops at meetings led to an interruption every 2 minutes (Rosen 2015).

Above and beyond the time it takes to respond to each of the digital distractions, it requires a tremendous amount of additional time (and brain energy) to return to where you were before being interrupted. For example, your child stops to read and answer a text. They may say that it only took 30 seconds to respond. However, the text interrupted their line of reasoning in the essay that they were in the process of writing. "Now, where was I? What was I thinking?" Re-orienting themselves may involve going back a bit in the essay and then figuring out again what comes next. Depending on the study, research shows that this re-orientation—just to get back to where you were—takes from 1–5 minutes to as long as 25 minutes.

In short, "Psychological research long ago proved what most of us know from experience: frequent interruptions scatter our thoughts, weaken our memory, and make us tense and anxious. The more complex the train of thought we're involved in, the greater the impairment the distractions cause" (Carr 2011, p.132).

Thus, attempts to "multi-task" during school work present a triple whammy: First, there is the time to answer the interruption. Second, there is the tremendously wasteful expenditure of time as the student returns to where they were before the interruption. Third, their brain is further slowed down by the energy and stress expended as the insula gets whiplash endeavoring to switch from one activity to another. Keep this in mind as you make arrangements with your child about distracting devices in their room during homework time (see Chapter 5).

"Multi-tasking" is inefficient, and thus actually decreases free time. Your child will have more free time and less stress if they put away their digital technology while studying.

"But Mom, it's so boring when I'm not playing video games": The need for down-time

Even though your child may be able to chew food (a pretty automatic task) and play Nintendo at the same time, and thus seem to "multi-task" fairly efficiently in this situation, the video game interferes with the brain's ability to lounge in down-time, which would have occurred if the child had just enjoyed the experience of eating while letting their mind wander or chatting with family. Down-time is important. As Gardner and Davis (2014, p.74) write:

> Daydreaming, wandering, and wondering have positive facets. Introspection may be particularly important for young people who are actively figuring out who and what they want to be... [W]ithout breaking away from an app-determined life path, young persons risk prematurely foreclosing their identities, making it less likely that they will achieve a fully realized and personally fulfilling sense of self.

Screens may also soak up time we might have invested in a nap. It has been well accepted that a nap of even 10–20 minutes improves cognitive function and vigor, as well as reducing sleepiness and fatigue. (Note, however, that people usually wake up feeling drowsy following a longer nap of 1 hour or more.)

Screens cut into time for unstructured play

Screen-time activities not only interfere with down-time, but also interfere with unstructured play. After reviewing decades of research, the American Academy of Pediatrics concluded that screenless, unstructured play provides the best avenue for young children to learn the skills of problem solving, reasoning, communication, creativity and motor skills. On behalf of the Academy, Dr Ari Brown concluded, "In today's 'achievement culture,' the best thing you can do for your young child is give her a chance to have unstructured play—both with you and independently. Children need this in order to figure out how the world works" (AAP 2011b).

Screens cut into time for other structured play and activities

Besides reducing down-time creative thinking, excessive media use also cuts into free time that could have been utilized for productive activities such as sports, music, drama, and learning how to get along with real-life people. ADHD kids, in particular, lose out on opportunities to practice controlling impulsivity, increasing attention, socialization, and self-control. In fact, video games by their very nature may actually reinforce those negative traits. (On the flip side, though, digital technology is the currency of much of a child's socialization with peers, and may thus have a beneficial social effect as well as possibly teaching certain skills such as reading.) There's more about the Internet and specific populations in Chapter 3.

Screens interfere with developing voluntary attention

Voluntary attention—the ability to willfully control where to focus your attention and thus control your actions—is a critical skill to master. It is, perhaps, the most important predictor of future success. This was demonstrated in the 1970s by the "marshmallow test" conducted at Stanford University. Young children were offered a treat, such as a marshmallow, and told that they could eat it right away; or, if they waited alone for 15 minutes, they would get *two* marshmallows. The majority of youngsters could endure only 3 minutes of waiting before digging in. However, 30% waited for the whole 15 minutes and received the double reward. These 30% used a variety of techniques to volitionally direct their attention away from the marshmallow in front of them: some covered their eyes, others sang songs, etc.

Here's the interesting part: Follow-up studies until age 40 showed that those children who could control their attention—wresting their attention away from the attractive stimuli—did better in multiple aspects of life, such as Scholastic Aptitude Test (SAT) scores, successful education, keeping friends, etc. Success in the marshmallow test was more predictive than any other test, including intelligence quotient (IQ). These findings have been repeatedly confirmed (Palladino 2015).

Thus, when we teach our kids to exercise self-control (volitional attention) to get off their screens, it is hoped that they are developing one of life's most important skills. It's okay that it requires work to get themselves out of the gravitational pull of the screen. This is a skill that is well worth mastering, despite the parent–child skirmishes that might result while it's developing.

Areas where digital learning does excel

Of course, there are areas where digital learning is advantageous:

- eReading saves paper.

- eReading may improve access to books and other information in areas with limited resources.

- Technologies enhanced by computers are appealing to students, and seem to keep them involved in learning that requires rehearsal/repetition. One meta-analysis of 46 studies (involving more than 36,000 students) showed "significant positive effects" in mathematics from computer use. Another meta-analysis of 84 studies (totaling more than 60,000 students) showed that computer programs designed to improve reading had a positive effect, albeit small, on reading skills. Importantly, all of these technologies were more effective with teacher support (Greenfield 2015).

• Special needs students show largely positive benefits from digital technologies. This includes children with dyslexia, visual impairment, autism spectrum disorders, and intellectual disability—improving either their ability to learn or to communicate (Greenfield 2015).

Summary of digital vs. print effects on learning

Here are my conclusions based on the above:

• Reading material digitally is probably fine for short texts that the reader doesn't plan on studying or otherwise re-reading.

• Many, but not all, studies suggest that hard copy is better than digital learning for longer texts, or texts that are to be studied or otherwise re-read.

• Digital reading is burdened by the requirement of a distracting digital device (leading to inefficient attempts at "multi-tasking"), poor ability to sense where the reader is in the text, and distracting hyperlinks that interrupt concentration and disrupt the author's carefully planned line of reasoning.

• Hard copy text is clearly preferred as a reading experience. Although as yet unproven, a more pleasurable reading experience may lead students to spend more time engaged with the text, thus resulting in better learning.

- Open laptops and smartphones are a huge distraction and are shown to negatively affect classroom attention and learning, even when being used to surf for material related to the classroom subject.

- Moderate use of technology, along with teacher supervision, appears to be useful, particularly for material requiring repetition/rehearsal and for special needs students.

- Final answers are not in yet. Maybe the youngest generation will be different. But even our high school and college students feel as above, and they are pretty much digital natives.

- Schools switching to all-digital communication may be well intentioned but the strategy could be counter-productive. We may need to wait until the students start their adult lives and careers to know which approach is best. In the meantime, when choices are available, do we really need to have our students spend even more time on a screen than their own inclinations already take them? Does having a screen open all day during class really help our kids to keep a digital balance in their life?

Other psychological effects of digital technology

In addition to effects on reading and other learning issues, there are other psychological effects of the Internet on its users. Gardner and Davis (2014) identify issues relating to identity formation, intimacy, and imagination.

Effects on identity

On the Internet, you can be whoever you want to be. You have time to shape your avatar however you wish. You can come up with those witty responses that you missed in real life. You can be strong. You can post on social media only the good things going on in your life. Your life can be perfect online.

Or, it can be hell. You may have created an online persona that doesn't reflect the real you, but you are now locked into it. The actions of others online may force you to adopt unwanted traits into your persona. Your sense of self-worth may depend upon how quickly other people respond to your postings and how many "likes" you get. It's a system that requires constant, time-consuming upkeep. More on this in Chapter 2.

Effects on intimacy

By virtue of multiple, real-time communication with others, digital technology opens previously unavailable methods of sharing with others, near and far, and thus can promote closeness and friendship.

Or not. Electronic communication may result in superficial relationships hampered by lack of face-to-face communication. Constant communication with a peer may seem—when each is viewed in isolation—as meaningless chatter ("Who cares what kind of hair-day you're having?"); but when taken in total, it can constitute a degree of detailed intimacy, even from afar.

Fortunately, research shows that "by and large, young people use online communication not merely to substitute for face-to-face communication, but rather to augment it... whereby the added opportunities to communicate with one's friends translate into increased feelings of closeness to them" (Gardner and Davis 2014, p.108).

Effects on imagination

Yet, again, depending on its use, digital technology can be either a boom or a bust when it comes to imagination and creativity. Apps and the Internet open new doors to creativity and collaboration (an important part of creativity); on the other hand, they can stifle creativity by encouraging mimicry, limited communication via tweets, or by providing distractions that limit time for creativity.

Association with other psychological conditions

Many studies show that excessive digital technology use is associated with a wide variety of psychological conditions. It is essential to note that for most of these associations, which is the cause and which is the effect have not been determined. For example, we know that depression is associated with extensive digital technology use. However, most current research can't distinguish whether an underlying initial depression came first and then led to Internet use as an escape, or whether the Internet use created enough problems in the life of a previously happy child to now make them depressed. The inability to distinguish cause and effect is a major problem in "observational studies." (Observational studies involve passive observation of whether two scenarios typically occur in the same population at any given time.)

However, observational studies are frequently all we have. It is often impossible and/or unethical to do the best kind of research, which is a randomized, prospective, double-blind study (in such a protocol, participants are randomly assigned to one of two or more groups at the onset of the study, and are then followed into the future to see what happens to each group— meanwhile neither the researchers nor the study participants know which group the participants have been assigned to). For example, what are the researchers supposed to do? Find 1000 teenagers, make half of them play video games for 5 hours/ day the other half never, then follow the kids into adulthood and see which group ends up more depressed? Would you sign your little prodigy up for such an experiment?

So, with that proviso in mind, the following psychological conditions have been associated with extensive use of digital technology:

- ADHD

- social communication problems

- ASD

- social anxiety

- anxiety/stress

- Obsessive/Compulsive Disorder

- depression

- relationship problems

- school problems

- substance abuse

- other behavioral addictions (e.g., food, sex, gambling).

Whenever evaluating someone for excessive digital technology use, we must also consider those associated psychological conditions.

Neurological effects of digital technology abuse

The human brain has a great deal of "plasticity"—in other words, it can remodel itself slowly on an evolutionary level, or much more rapidly on an individual level. For example, primitive brain circuits that were originally helpful in visual recognition have been reshaped into a specialized area capable of reading; and primitive brain circuits that were originally used by the brain for numerical functions have been "recycled" for higher arithmetic. Additionally, the development of deep reading skills is associated with further extensive brain changes as each child learns to read.

In this section, I examine some of the neurological effects associated with digital technology abuse, focusing primarily on brain imaging studies. Once again, the cause vs. effect of these associations has usually not been determined. Also, it's not clear that these changes are necessarily bad. For example, as we learn to read, our brain undergoes changes, but that's a good thing. Here's a sampling of what else has been revealed. Even if we can't determine cause/effect, the association of "hard scientific findings" on magnetic resonance imaging (MRI) adds to the credibility of the existence of the problems we have been discussing. A complete summary of neuroimaging studies of Internet addiction can be found in Lin and Lei (2015).

- An MRI study shows a correlation between media "multi-tasking" with smaller anterior corpus callosum volumes.

- "Multi-tasking" with action video games correlates with functional and structural changes in the frontoparietal attention network, and produces improvements in certain kinds of attention.

- Internet addiction is correlated with changes in parts of the brain controlling self-control and recognition of rewards at appropriate levels.

(Loh 2015)

- Nuclear studies show abnormal dopamine regulation in the prefrontal cortex seen in Internet addiction. This could explain the excessive reward perceived by the person with the addiction, as well as their inability to control the behavior.

- Brain scans show similar changes between video game addiction and changes seen in other forms of addiction. Similarities exist both structurally and regarding dopamine reward system findings.

(Huang 2015)

In summary, brain imaging studies show that, compared to the general population, people with an Internet addiction have decreased gray matter in areas of the brain that are responsible for cognitive control, inhibition of incorrect responses, execution of goal-directed behavior, motivation, and reward processing. Imaging studies also reveal white matter (the connecting highways between areas of the brain) differences in areas that control memory and multi-sensory input (Yuan *et al.* 2011). Although the severity of these changes correlates with the duration of the addictive symptoms, it remains unclear as to whether these changes are the cause or the result of Internet addiction. Regardless, the data help to verify a true biological underpinning of the addictive spiral—perhaps helping caregivers to become more empathic to those afflicted by addiction.

Physical effects of digital media use

Somewhat surprisingly—or not—there are multiple physical effects and dangers associated with digital media use and abuse:

- *Poor sleep and daytime sleepiness.* Even the light emanating from a laptop screen can prevent the brain's secretion of melatonin, a natural hormone released in darkness that instructs the brain to go to sleep. In a survey of 3076 Swiss 8th-graders, children with problematic Internet use were more than two times as likely to have sleep problems than average Internet users (Suris *et al.* 2014). Using yellow sunglasses (available through Amazon) helps to filter out the part of the light spectrum that interferes with sleep onset.

- *Backaches, musculoskeletal pain, and headaches* appear to be additional issues mediated by these sleep problems (Suris *et al.* 2014).

- *Aggression* is self-reported even by typical childhood users, even after as little as 30 minutes of technology use (Smahel, Wright and Cernikova 2015).

- *Poor eating habits, including skipped meals and obesity.* The latter appears to be associated with a TV in the child's room—along with *substance abuse, smoking, and exposure to pornography* (AAP 2013).

- *Injury from texting while driving.* It takes an average of 5 seconds to even glance at a text, during which time a car moving at 60 miles per hour will have traveled much more than the length of a football field. Think it doesn't still happen? Almost half of US high-schoolers had read or sent a text/email while driving in the past 30 days. Think it's only teens? The percentage still holds at 31% of US drivers aged 18–64 (Burley Hofmann 2014).

- *Injuries from texting while walking.* It turns out that texting while walking results in more injuries per mile than those that result from distracted driving, albeit these pedestrian accidents are typically less severe. Emergency room visits related to cell phone use at Ohio State University tripled between 2004 and 2010. Of the tens of thousands of ER visits for pedestrian accidents occurring yearly in the US, some 10% are considered to be related to cell phone use while walking (*Science Daily* 2014; Glatter 2012).

- *Hearing loss* due to noise exposure has been found in 12.5% of US children aged 6–19. Earphones, powered by portable music players, are among the chief suspects. After all, with earphones on, you can play music all day long, and no parent can detect the volume and scream, "Turn that thing down!" Children and adolescents need routine hearing screening to prevent or mitigate hearing loss (Kennedy Krieger Institute 2015).

- *Repetitive movement thumb injuries* from all of that texting (Eapen *et al.* 2014). Also, what's going to happen to our kids' necks/posture from spending all of those hours with their neck flexed downward while they stare at the screen in their lap?

- *Hypercholesterolemia, hypertension, and asthma* are associated (not necessarily caused by) heavy television use (Strasburger, Jordan and Donnerstein 2010).

- *Deaths and injuries from falling digital TVs.* Each year, a multitude of children die or are injured by toppling large flat-screen televisions and/or the furniture that they rest on. Young children often pull out a drawer in order to climb up onto furniture and can be crushed and injured (especially neurologically) by the resultant falling stand or TV. Often they are attempting to reach the remote control or other goodie on the TV or its stand. TVs need to be securely fastened to the wall with readily available tethers. Do not store the remote or other attractive items on or near the TV. Low, wide-based furniture is less likely to tip. For more information, see the Products Safety Project (2015).

- *"Death by selfie"* refers to the dozens of people who have been killed by placing themselves in risky positions while attempting to photograph themselves. More people die each year from selfies than from shark attacks. Mumbai has banned selfies after 19 deaths in India were attributed to them. Deaths have occurred from falling off cliffs, being hit by a train, car accidents, and shooting oneself while posing with one's own gun. (Apparently, guns don't kill people…selfies do.) Further, it is feared that taking selfies interferes with actually experiencing and living in the moment of that special event (Salie 2016).

Chapter 2

PROBLEMS WITH THE *CONTENT* OF DIGITAL TECHNOLOGY

In Chapter 1, we examined problems with the *use* of the Internet/digital technology—problems associated with the technology itself as the vessel through which we communicate. We discussed such issues as the effects on reading caused by hyperlinks and "multi-tasking," along with the brain changes and physical problems associated with Internet use. In Chapter 2, we turn our attention to the actual *content* delivered via that conduit of digital technology.

Of course, terrific information and social opportunities are made instantly available through the Internet. Few of us, if any, would give it up for either ourselves or our children—not that we have a choice. The Internet is here to stay. We can't, nor do we want to, prevent our children from participating in the digital age.

There are, of course, a whole host of dangers that we allow our children to be exposed to online, including ones used by "typical" children in "typical" amounts. Most parents don't monitor the lyrics or content of the media that their children consume. Then, there are the online dangers of giving out too much personal information, sexting and bullying—irresponsible behaviors made easier by the perception that one can't be seen or see the recipient. Lest we think that it couldn't happen to our own little angels, in fact 64% of teenagers admit to online behaviors that their parents would disapprove of, and 81% of adults don't trust their children online.

We'll look at issues related to:

- Social media:
  - bullying
  - sexting
  - privacy
- Digital media such as lyrics and videos
- Digital games:
  - role-playing games
  - violence
- Pornography.

Social media

As we have seen, a great deal of social communication is done on the Internet. To review:

- 71% of children have a TV or Internet device in their room, thereby granting them continuous access to digital media (AAP 2013).

- 62% of iGeneration (teen) students state that they check their digital devices more frequently than every 15 minutes (Rosen 2012).

- Teens received and sent 3705 texts/month—about 6/hour (Rosen 2012).

- 1 in 3 teens sends more than 100 texts/day (largely replacing phone use) (AAP 2013).

- Facebook had 1.19 billion users in 2013, 50% of whom log in daily (Griffiths, Kuss and Demetrovics 2014).

- Yet, 2 out of 3 children and teens say that their parents have no media rules. It's the "Wild West" out there of frequently unsupervised social and other activities (AAP 2013).

The appeal of social media
You can re-invent, or airbrush, your life

There is a *New Yorker* magazine cartoon where one dog is typing at the computer, while looking over to another canine stating, "On the Internet, no one knows you're a dog." Indeed, on the Internet, you can present yourself however you wish. You can re-invent yourself, presenting only the good parts and the good times. You can "airbrush" your entire life—not only your photographs, but your entire existence. Edit out the bad times, embellish the best. Somehow, "selfies" seem to portray only the good times. Your life seems wonderful.

Unfortunately, it's a hard, time-consuming image to keep up, and the constant documentation of life through selfies and tweets may interfere with actually living it. "Okay," you might think, "I've gotten my selfie in front of the Grand Canyon. Let's go, already!"

Further, the constant presentation of the idealized self may make it harder to reveal your true self, with all of its doubts, frailties, and anxieties. The real you may find itself taken over by your virtual image. It also makes others suffer from "FOMO"—Fear of Missing Out—of all of those good times that their peers seem to be having. "My life seems to be so dull and unpopular compared to everyone else's. I'm not always having that much fun." We need to explain this to our children, and admit that we often feel that way, too—for example, at parties where we briefly catch up with associates who tell us wonderful things about their family, or when we receive those holiday greeting cards, where everyone seems to be so happy. We don't often get a card that says "Season's greetings. My son may be smiling in this photo, but he just got out of rehab."

"Likes" are addictive

In the "good old days," you earned positive feedback slowly through good deeds or other accomplishments. With the advent of social media, our children become impatient for an immediate answer or "Like" within minutes of sending that urgent piece of information out, either as a text to one person, a group text, the hundreds of "friends" they've amassed, or the entire world. "I just have to check again to see if anyone has responded, yet." Every positive response gives a small drop of dopamine right into the brain's reward center. Even more powerfully, neuroimaging studies reveal that the *anticipation* of a reward is more stimulating than its actual receipt. Plus, the reward from each response is not enough to be totally satisfying, leaving you still hungry for more—another feature of addictive behavior (Greenfield 2015). Thus, the ability to present yourself as you wish plus the dopamine reward of the instant feedback both contribute to the time spent on social media.

Cyber-bullying

Of course, not all responses are positive. Oftentimes, people re-invent themselves as "cool" (often meaning "cruel"). Cyber-bullying is when digital technology is used to embarrass, intimidate, threaten, harass, or tease someone else. Of course, the Internet didn't invent bullying, but its ability to spread taunts rapidly to others and the apparent anonymity or lack of face-to-face exposure required to say mean things may make it easier. Groups can be set up easily to entice others to join in. This has led to widespread meanness in social media. In a survey of US girls aged 12 or 13, 1 in 3 said that interactions on social networking sites were "mostly unkind" (Greenfield 2015). That exposure not only nicks away at our children's self-image, but also teaches them by example that cruelty is an acceptable norm.

It is part of our job as parents to explicitly teach that cruelty is not acceptable in any environment—whether it's virtual or the real physical world. We need to teach our children how to resolve conflict. You can bring up the topic by casually asking if anything online is bothering them. Explain that if disputes are handled in person, they are less likely to spread digitally. Burley Hofmann (2014, p.55) suggests writing, "I don't want to talk about this online." In any case, teach the "Five-Minute Rule," where you wait 5 minutes before hitting the send button when being defensive, offensive, or aggressive. Sometimes, it's even better to "sleep on it" in such situations. Burley Hofmann also suggests blocking out those people who are harassing you. Facebook has information on dealing with bullying, as does www.stopbullying.org and your school's psychologist or guidance counselor. The topic will be explored in Chapter 4.

Sexting

Like it or not, many of our kids are sending or receiving personal sexual images. Most of these photos are sent deliberately, although some are sent out accidentally to unintended recipients, and on occasion as "revenge porn," designed to express anger or get even.

- A survey of 600 southwest high-school students found that almost 1 in 5 participants had sent sexually explicit pictures of themselves over their mobile phone. Of these students, more than 1 in 3 was aware of potential legal or other serious repercussions.

- Almost 2 out of 5 students in that survey said they had received a sexually explicit image on their phone. Of these students, more than a quarter had forwarded such pictures to others.

(Steiner-Adair and Barker 2013)

But everybody is doing it

No, everybody isn't. The majority of kids are not sexting. If your child receives a sext, teach them "delete and don't repeat." They can turn down a request for sexting by diverting the suggestion with humor, keeping it offline, and resisting falling for the line, "I'll show you mine if you show me yours." Unfortunately, a double standard exists between boys and girls, where girls are exposed to much greater consequences than boys. It is not an even trade.

Our youth need to know that even if you are under 18 and you create, send, or receive sexually explicit images of another minor, it could be considered child pornography under current US federal law. This even includes taking a picture of yourself, or of another consenting minor. (Since minors can't give legal consent for naked pictures, there is no such thing as a consenting minor.) Sexting laws in your state can be found at http://mobilemediaguard.com/state_main.html.

Make sure that your child knows that you won't go totally ballistic if they inform you about such things. Of course, you'll be disappointed and angry, but they need to know that you won't add to the drama unnecessarily, and they can always come to you for help. The website www.commonsensemedia.org has good advice.

Giving out too much information

Studies show that almost 50% of teens have revealed personal information, such as physical descriptions or photos, to strangers. More than half send out group messages to all of their Facebook friends, which averages out to more than 500 people at once for the typical youth (Greenfield 2015). Heaven knows where the information goes from there. Our kids need to learn that there is no such thing as privacy on the Internet. Even on Snapchat. Ever heard of screen shot, or the forward button? Parental controls can be applied. Facebook privacy settings can be adjusted. Good suggestions can also be found in *The Smart Girl's Guide to Privacy* by V. Blue, as well as in the Resources section at the end of this book.

Before sending out any information, the senders should ask themselves:

- Will this image/information get me or someone else in trouble?

- Do I have consent to tag the person in the photo?

- Will this image/information cause drama?

- Do I remember that it might get passed on to anyone?

- Would my grandmother approve of me sending it?

- How will I feel a year from now?

- Am I sending this to true friends, or are they just added to my "friends" list so I can seem more popular. Would they stand by me if something went wrong?

Hiding too much information

It's hard to keep up with devious behavior, especially with people who are more comfortable with tech skills than we are. Prime examples are what are called "Vault apps," which appear to be innocent apps, but enter the right passcode and they lead to privately stored images and/or other hidden materials. For example, one app looks like a regular calculator app. Open it, and there's a calculator. However, enter the passcode and, voilà, access to the hidden material is granted. Some apps even have a decoy password, so if a parent asks for the vault's password they can be led to a decoy stash of innocent stuff.

Parents can take proactive measures. Set controls so that their child's smartphone requires the parent's approval anytime the child wants to download an app, whether paid for or free. Information regarding this for iPhones can be found on the Apple website, and requires setting up each iPhone with Family Sharing and then turning on the Ask to Buy feature on the child's phone. Android users can set parental controls on Google Play's app store. The Android app called AppLock can be applied to apps suspected of being vaults, locking them down with a PIN code. See also www.commonsensemedia.org, www.teensafe.com, and http://safetynet.aap.org.

The good part of social media

Of course, there are good parts of social media. It makes it easy to keep up with family and true friends. Studies show that online communication and self-disclosure can improve teenagers' connections socially, with a subsequent improved sense of well-being. However, this beneficial result only occurs with real friends and family. When communication techniques are used with strangers, they tend to result in a diminished sense of being socially connected (Strasburger *et al.* 2010).

Even the constant tweeting about minutiae such as "I'm wearing the funky pink skirt today" can have a positive effect, whereupon the sum of the whole is greater than its individual parts. Taken cumulatively over weeks and months, the tidbits of information weave a portrait of your friend's inner life. You know the person. You know their routine. You may feel surprisingly close.

Does exposure to pornography and other media affect sexuality?

Yes. The sex drive is normal and important to the survival of any species, including ours. It's natural. What isn't natural is the depiction of sexual "norms" so readily available to our kids. Internet pornography doesn't typically reflect real-life sexual activity. Not only does it ignore so-called "old-fashioned" ideas about needing to care about and/or love your sexual partner, exposure to pornography raises unrealistic expectations of what people will experience in their actual lives. Youth don't know that this stuff is just fantasy—demeaning fantasy that typically doesn't model respect, affection, or safe-sex practices. Looking at your father's *Playboy* is nothing like the material available to our children now. Open discussion about sex and pornography is required, or else our kids will rely on the Internet for their sexual advice. Sexual information from porn sites or from us—which will it be? Hint: porn sites pay a whole lot better than parenting, so the sites aren't going away.

Let's look at some actual facts and conclusions provided by the American Academy of Pediatrics (2010) in their article, "Policy Statement—Sexuality, Contraception, and the Media." We will examine the state of sexuality in the US, the extent of media exposure to sex in the US, and then examine the relationship between the two.

Teenage sexuality in the US

- 46% of high-school seniors have had sexual intercourse.

- 14% of high-school seniors have had at least four partners.

- 10% of young women who had sex in their teen years stated that their first time was involuntary.

- Centers for Disease Control and Prevention data show that 1 in 4 teenagers has had a sexually transmitted infection.

- At the time of writing, the US still has the highest teen pregnancy rate in the Western world.

(AAP 2010)

Teenage exposure to sexual content in US media

- *Television.* US children and adolescents spent 7 hours/day on media, with TV the most predominant. 75% of prime time shows had sexual content. However, only very infrequently (14%) did the show mention any of the risks or responsibilities involved with sex.

- *Music.* 40% of lyric lines contained sexual material; only 6% gave healthy messages about sex.

- *Movies.* Teen movies contained distorted views of romance and normal adolescent activities. Almost all R-rated teen movies contained at least one nude scene.

- *Internet.* A 2007 national survey of 10–17-year-olds revealed that almost half had viewed pornography online in the past year.

- *Overall,* a 1999 survey of over 2000 girls aged 11–17 years, revealed that only the 11-year-olds didn't feel media-related pressure to start having sex.

(AAP 2010)

The relationship between media exposure and adolescent sexual behavior

Correlational studies demonstrate that at a given single "snapshot" of time, two factors tend to run together—they correlate with each other, but don't prove that either factor causes the other. For example, blue eyes and blonde hair run together (correlate), but neither causes the other. Correlational studies have reached the following associations:

- Listening to sexually degrading lyrics is associated with earlier intercourse.

- Exposure to rap music videos or pornography is associated with the chance of developing a sexually transmitted disease or of having multiple partners in black female teenagers.

• Exposure to media with sexual content increases the intention to have sex in the near future.

• TV in a child's bedroom is associated with greater sexual activity and drug use by teenagers.

(AAP 2010)

Longitudinal studies are those that follow a group over time, and thus can give stronger evidence of possible cause and effect. Longitudinal studies seem to implicate sexy media leading to earlier sex.

• Multiple studies show that exposure to TV and other media with sexual content doubles the risk of early sexual intercourse, especially among white teens.

• Adolescents are less likely to engage in early sex when their parents limit their TV viewing.

• The risk of teen pregnancy is doubled with early exposure to sexual content.

• Importantly, research has also shown that TV programs *can* be a force for good, by raising awareness about sexually related issues, and by providing education and an opening of discussion between youth and their parents.

(AAP 2010)

Does media exposure increase the risk of violent behavior?

Yes. The answer, based on an overwhelming predominance of research, shows a definite association between violence presented digitally and aggressive, violent behavior. The evidence is close to conclusive that the media exposure actually is causative, not merely statistically associated. These conclusions were reached by an American Academy of Pediatrics (AAP 2009a) policy statement on media violence, which referenced similar conclusions by the National Institute of Mental Health (NIMH) and the Federal Communications Commission (FCC).

- *Television* still shares much of the blame, made worse by the frequent placement of a TV in the child's room (19% of infants and 68% of children 8 years or older have a TV in their bedroom). A TV in a child's bedroom increases their exposure to TV by 1 hour/day. A large proportion of TV content is now consumed by smartphone or other computer-related screen. Media consumes so much of a child's life that it is replacing parents and teachers as role models. Bedroom access to such technology makes it harder for parents to monitor what the kids are watching—much of their viewing is of a violent nature. It has been estimated that violence on TV has been viewed 200,000 times by the time our children reach the age of 18 years. That exposure frequently demonstrates the use of violence and guns as a means of conflict resolution (AAP 2009a).

- *Movies* also contribute to exposure to violence—100% of US animated movies released from 1937 to 1999 showed violence, with an ever-rising portrayal of violence with intent to harm (AAP 2009a).

- *Musical lyrics* also play a role in media's contribution to violence exposure. The average US youth listens to music 1.5–2.5 hours/day, with "at-risk" youth listening to music almost 7 hours/day. Much of this listening is done through earbuds, reducing parents' ability to monitor the music (AAP 2009b). (Parents can find the lyrics to their child's music by using one of the sites that come up on a search of "music lyrics.")

Do violent video games lead to violent behavior?

Yes. There is strong evidence that playing violent video games (which represent 60% of video game sales) leads to aggressive behavior. An exhaustive meta-analysis of 381 tests on over 130,000 participants found that violent video games significantly increased aggressive cognition, aggressive behavior, and physical arousal, while they decreased sensitivity to violence and positive social interaction (Greenfield 2015). Video games present an ideal place to rehearse violence, starting with the provocation, followed by the creation and the execution of violence as a means of conflict resolution. Indeed, violence is rewarded with points or moving up a level (Greenfield 2015). Quite a number of laboratory studies confirm that violent video games make us react with greater aggression. What is less clear, though, is how long these effects last, and whether they invariably carry over into natural scenarios. So far, no studies demonstrate a direct lead to criminal-level violence (Greenfield 2015). Let's look at a few of the studies upon which such conclusions are based.

In one study, teenage boys were assigned to play a realistically violent video game (you know the sort, with blood flying all over the place), a fantasy game containing violence, or a non-violent video game. After playing, they competed with a partner on a non-video task. The winner of the task was told that he could play loud noises through the loser's headphones—and was wrongly told that the noise could cause permanent hearing loss. Those who had played a violent game were the most aggressive in the use of the loud noise on a partner with whom they had no grudge. Realistic violence and being immersed in the video game were particular risk factors for subsequent aggressive behavior (Greenfield 2015).

In another study, students were randomly assigned to play a violent or a non-violent video game. Then, a fake fight was staged outside the lab. Students who had just finished playing the violent game were less likely to respond quickly and help, to judge the fight as serious, or even to hear the fight. It seems in this lab experiment that the violent video game desensitized the player to violence (Greenfield 2015).

In another study, subjects were randomly assigned to play a violent or non-violent video game for 20 minutes. They were then all shown a film clip of graphic real-world violent behavior. Those who had just played the violent video game showed less reactivity to the horror on the film clip, as measured by less increase in heart rate and sweating measured by skin conductance (Greenfield 2015).

Gaming was also associated with less activity from a region of the brain involved in emotionally charged memory, called the amygdala (Greenfield 2015).

Certainly, though, there are some positive skills that can be learned from all of that practice involved in playing video games. Controlled studies have shown that gaming results in better visual–spatial skills, eye–hand coordination, ability to notice and track multiple simultaneous creatures, notice small details, and switch flexibly between tasks. In fact, gamers make quite good laparoscopic surgeons (Greenfield 2015).

Does media affect substance use?

Yes. 70% of movies made in 2010 still contained smoking, without any mention of its negative effects. Does this affect children's smoking habits? Yes. Studies show that exposure to movies with smoking during grades 5–8 predicts starting to smoke 1–8 years later. Similar statements can be made about alcohol use (Strasburger *et al.* 2010).

Resultant American Academy of Pediatrics recommendations regarding digital media

- Media including TV, smartphones, music lyrics, and music videos all contribute to effects on sexuality and violence. This should be discussed with your doctor.

- Limit total entertainment screen time to less than 1–2 hours/day.

- Do not allow TV or Internet-connected devices in the child's bedroom. A TV in the child's bedroom makes it harder to monitor what they are watching, has been found to increase a child's exposure to TV by 1 hour/day, is associated with worse school performance, raises the risk of smoking by a factor of two, and the risk of obesity rises by 31%. The latter is probably related to commercials pushing poor food choices and there is also the possibility of a decrease in physical exercise.

- Monitor the child's media and the websites they visit.

- Co-view media with your child and teen. This is for their safety and also to open up discussions.

- Set up a family plan.

(AAP 2013)

- Model good media behavior. Studies show that the heavy media use of parents is the strongest predictor of heavy media use in their children. Parental discussion of issues presented by media has been found to be successful in countering the effects of harmful content, including children being less likely to engage in risky sexual behaviors (Strasburger *et al.* 2010).

Note that a more recent (2015) American Academy of Pediatrics' set of "talking points" (which are not yet codified into an official policy statement) is de-emphasizing specific time limits in favor of the following types of suggestions:

- The digital world is just another environment, where children can do in a virtual (digital) environment the same things that they have always done—both good and bad. Parents have the same duties regarding all environments: teaching kindness, setting limits (kids need and want them), knowing where their children are going, what they will be doing, and with whom, etc. Would you let your child go out into the real world without asking them about their plans?

- The quality of the content is more important than the time spent on it. Make sure that your child is prioritizing how they spend their time, rather than simply setting a timer.

- Make time for your child to interact with you. Set aside time for structured play (with and without you), as well as for unstructured play and other interests. Does the screen time help or interfere with other activities?

- Establish tech-free zones during meals and night-time. Use a central location for overnight charging of devices.

- Talk-time with the child is critical for language development, and requires two-way communication. Live interaction is best. Optimal educational media exposure begins after the age of 2 years. Before that age, media just tends to cut into time devoted to parental/child communication.

- Co-engagement of media by parents is essential for infants and toddlers, and helps learning and social interaction with all children.

(Brown, Shifrin and Hill 2015)

I will post an updated summary of these recommendations on my website www.KidsBehavioralNeurology.com when they have been revised and are published as the "official policy" of the American Academy of Pediatrics. See more on these and additional suggestions in Chapters 4 and 5.

Chapter 3

PROBLEMS REGARDING SPECIFIC POPULATIONS

In this chapter, we turn our attention to screen-time issues as they relate to three particular groups, notably:

- very young children (especially those younger than 2 years old)

- children with ADHD

- children with an ASD.

As we shall see, digital technology has not been demonstrated to be useful to very young children, and may even be detrimental to their language, cognition, and attention. Children with ADHD may be excessively drawn to media, which rewards their impulsivity and task-switching behaviors—things we are otherwise trying to correct. ADHD children are also much more prone to an Internet addiction. People on the autism spectrum may find the interface of the screen less stressful than face-to-face communication. As such, social media and texting may be a boon to practicing socialization skills, but also puts people on the autism spectrum at risk of withdrawing into their online virtual world.

Very young children and screen time
Statistics on usage

Despite the American Academy of Pediatrics' (AAP 2011a) discouragement of screen time for children younger than 2 years of age, 90% of such children have some type of screen time. In fact, the average child under 2 years old watches television for 1–2 hours/day. This does not include exposure to 4 hours or more of "background" TV, where the adult has the TV on— whether paying attention to it or not. Although 40% of parents watch the media with their child, many times screens are used to give the parent the freedom to do other chores or activities (AAP 2011a). A more recent set of AAP "talking points" (Brown *et al.* 2015) seems to soften the discouragement of use by children less than 2 years of age, by instead emphasizing the need for live parental interaction and the essential need for co-viewing, and by stating that "optimum educational media exposure" starts after the age of 2 years.

It turns out that since the human brain triples in size over the first couple of years of life, there is plenty of reason to be concerned about the amount of time spent on screens during this period. However, time is not the only factor to be considered when discussing childhood screen usage. Attention must also be paid to the content of what is being watched, including quick screen shifts, rapid auditory editing, and flashing lights. In addition, there is the context of the exposure—in other words, how the child watches it. Context includes taking into consideration whether the child is watching alone, instead of forming language connections and bonds with family and peers. Context also includes consideration of what the child isn't doing, such as unstructured free time and experiencing books. All of this has to take into account the appropriateness of the material, given the stages of childhood brain development (Christakis 2009).

Is there any benefit to screen time for children less than 2 years old?

Not that we know of. Educational claims of screen-time activity for children less than 2 years old remain unproven, despite the enticing names of the programs and testimonials. Even studies of 2-year-olds watching high-quality educational programs such as *Sesame Street* have found either no effect or even a negative effect. Indeed, a study of 1000 children less than 2 years old could find no benefit from baby DVDs promising to improve language, and many of the infants actually had transient poorer language development (Christakis 2009). Such young children do not have the cognitive development to understand and pay attention to screen images. In particular, children do not typically develop the ability to follow a storyline sequentially from one scene to another until 12 months of age. Most children do not pay attention to television until 18 months of age.

To make matters worse, screen time at a young age takes away time from learning from real, live sources of information. From 12–18 months of age, material from a live presentation is more likely to be learned and retained than when it comes via a screen. Infants clearly learn language better from a live person speaking with them than from watching someone on TV or other media (Christakis 2009). Young children aged 12–36 months of age have been shown in multiple studies to also learn imitation and problem solving more effectively when they observe real-life demonstrations vs. watching the exact same demonstration on a video screen. This has been labeled the "video deficit." It seems that real people, who are physically present and paying attention, are most effective at engaging an infant's learning centers—especially if the infant has formed a bond with them (Steiner-Adair and Barker 2013). Perhaps this is partly due to the important role that interpersonal relationships play in driving language development. Watching a video is not reciprocal socialization: the baby doesn't need to talk back, and the baby can't form a bond with the video.

What about 3–5-year-olds?

There is a sharp contrast between the cognitive skills of infants and slightly older children, aged 3–5 years. For this latter age group, research has shown that high-quality educational programs such as *Sesame Street, Barney, Dora the Explorer, Blue's Clues,* and *Mister Rogers* help to improve language, social skills, and school readiness, which may persist into adolescence (Guernsey 2012).

Does "background" or "second-hand" TV interfere with child development?

It has been found that 39% of families with young children or infants have the television constantly on, during which period the youngster is in the room for more than half the time. The child may not be able to pay full attention to the adult material being played on the TV, but it exposes them to less than appropriate material, and perhaps most importantly, distracts the parent from interacting with their child. Background TV has been shown to affect not just the quantity of parental interactions, but also the quality (Guernsey 2012). Since the development of children's vocabulary is directly related to the amount of time parents spend speaking to them, background TV can inadvertently interfere with language development. Similarly, a child's time spent on their own digital device interferes with adult interaction and thus impedes the best way of developing language.

A child exposed to heavy family media also has less time devoted to unstructured playtime—which is fundamental to encouraging creativity and problem-solving skills. Children learn through trial and error, and through direct exploration of the people and things around them in a multi-sensory environment. The connection that a child feels with their parents and the parents' participation in their child's play is also essential. According to the American Academy of Pediatrics, "[t]he importance of parents sitting down to play with their children cannot be overstated" (AAP 2011a). Passively watching TV can't match bi-directional interaction between an infant and the people they care about and who care for them.

In addition, families with heavy media use spend significantly less time reading to their children, and the children spend less time reading by themselves. Turning distractions off and reading to your child fosters their language and thinking skills. Let them cuddle into your lap and read, laugh, and even cry together. Try to avoid reading together on a digital tablet, or you might find yourself dealing out a bunch of directions, such as "Don't push that!" instead of talking about the story and its meaning. Touch screens are appealing to the very young since they eliminate the need to dexterously use a mouse. That increased usability may not be a good thing; real people teach best.

In short, heavy media usage by the family may interfere with a child's development by reducing parents' time talking to, reading to, and playing with their child, as well as cutting into the child's own unstructured playtime and reading.

What are the short-term effects of these media issues? Several studies have associated heavy television use with language delay, especially if the child watches the screen alone. Again, these are studies that cannot separate cause and effect. Is it that TV causes language delay, or is it that language delay leads to the child being plopped in front of the TV more frequently by their parents in the hope that it will enrich their delayed child's speech? Conclusions about the long-term effects of early media use cannot yet be reached with available studies, but are an area of significant concern.

Am I really harming my infant if they have occasional screen time?

Guernsey (2012) summarizes the issue as follows: In the real world, parents do use media as a babysitter, and quite understandably so. Perhaps that break allows the parents to recoup, and thus be better parents. The child's developmental stage, the content, and the context of the media experience all need to be considered. Having taken these things into consideration, no one can say that moderated use of media is going to cause irreparable harm to your little one. Just make sure that they still get plenty of your attention, time, conversation, and play.

Children with ADHD and screen time
ADHD traits that make screen time so appealing

ADHD is officially defined as a combination of inattention/disorganization and/or hyperactivity/impulsivity. Currently recognized traits of ADHD also include executive function difficulties such as difficulty controlling where to shine your focus of attention, decreased ability to inhibit distractions, trouble with foresight and hindsight, and increased need for immediate feedback and reward.

Parents in my office almost universally exclaim, "I know that Johnny can't have ADHD... He can play video games forever!" However, ADHD doesn't mean you can't pay attention at all. It just means that you can't pay attention to anything except what is the most interesting stimulus available. In other words, people with ADHD cannot inhibit the most fascinating thing so that they can turn their attention to the most important thing. They are like moths that are always attracted to the brightest light and will stay there until something brighter (more attractive) comes along. (Unfortunately, sometimes the brightest light turns out to be a bug zapper!)

Let's use this expanded concept of ADHD to see how people with ADHD are at increased risk of falling prey to excessive media/video game use and even abuse:

- Video games are a very bright light, certainly much brighter than algebra homework or college entrance exams coming up in two years.

- Video games feature movement, and the human brain evolutionarily evolved to pay attention to movement in our environment.

- Video games are thus naturally attractive courtesy of our sensory/warning attention system, and don't require the forced volitional attention effort of other less interesting activities.

- Video games are constantly changing, fitting in with the ADHD trait of frequently shifting activities.

- Video games provide immediate feedback.

- Video games require an immediate reaction.

- Video games provide frequent but not totally satisfying hits of dopamine into our pleasure/reward centers.

- Video games have levels, with a bigger dopamine hit as we progress.

- Video games don't require writing, which is frequently a problem for those with ADHD.

- Online video games are social activities where people with ADHD may be more socially accepted than in the real world.

- All of the above may lead to excessive use of media/ video games, which leads to poor functioning in the real world, which leads to further escape into the world of gaming, where the person thinks they are achieving success. The cycle may spiral out of control.

The risk of ADHD and excessive Internet/gaming use

This excessive use of media/video games places people with ADHD at as high as a 25% risk of developing an Internet addiction, which is much higher than the control population.

Studies show that children prone to ADHD do not actually use the games more frequently or for longer. Rather, the difficulty seems to be the ADHD inability to control the drive and its resultant problems (Weiss *et al.* 2011). Of course, ADHD is not the only condition that raises the risk for excessive media use. Depression, anxiety, social phobia, hostility, the presence of other addictions, and—as we shall see shortly—ASDs also increase the risk (Weiss *et al.* 2011).

Further evidence for a connection between gaming and ADHD comes from a fascinating study of 62 children with ADHD and an Internet addiction who had never been treated with medication for ADHD before. Interestingly, an 8-week treatment with methylphenidate (the generic name for Ritalin) led to reduction of both their ADHD scores as well as their Internet addiction scores, and time spent on their screens (Weiss *et al.* 2011).

Clearly, the above study shows that ADHD and Internet addiction are related. That relationship is probably bi-directional: ADHD symptoms make gaming more attractive, and conversely, gaming exacerbates the ADHD symptoms. Gaming, unfortunately, reinforces just the kind of behaviors that we would like to eliminate in our children with ADHD: their quick and impulsive responses, acting before having a chance to think or use words, lack of patience, need for immediate reward, need for constantly changing stimuli, etc. Even worse, time spent on video games takes away time for other activities that could have otherwise helped to work on needed skills such as impulse control, volitional attention control, and relating to others. Such alternative activities include organized sports, joining clubs, making music, or spending time on the arts.

Although parents often think that their ADHD child excels at video games, research shows that ADHD is typically still an impairment to their video game performance. Actually, it's not that the ADHD child does better than their peers at video games, it's that they do better at video games than they do on their other activities (Weiss *et al.* 2011). Sorry.

Thus, given the strong natural attraction of individuals with ADHD to the fast-paced, rapidly rewarding aspects of gaming—along with the games' reinforcement of ADHD's negative traits—we need to be extra careful about the possibility for their development of excessive Internet/gaming use. We should also point out the risks of their impulsive and near-sighted behavior as it relates to all of the other dangers on the Internet, such as giving out too much personal information, sexting, pornography, gambling, and online purchases (including buying stuff to feed video game usage). See Chapter 4 for suggestions to help prevent/treat these problems.

Children with ASD and screen time
ASD traits that make screen time so appealing

The diagnosis of ASD is based on two general categories of symptoms. Here is a simplified presentation of the American Psychiatric Association's diagnostic criteria as outlined in the fifth edition (2013) of the *Diagnostic and Statistical Manual of Mental Disorders (DSM-5)*:

- *Trouble with back-and-forth reciprocal social interaction and social communication.* This can be further broken down into three areas:

  o *Problems with social and emotional reciprocity* (i.e., the ability to share ideas, emotions and thoughts with others and to engage others).

  o *Problems with non-verbal communication skills*, such as body language, eye contact and understanding hidden messages. These skills are necessary for social and emotional reciprocity.

  o *Problems with understanding, forming, and maintaining relationships.* Such problems may range from relative lack of urge to form bonds, diminished social pretend play, and knowing how to adjust your behavior according to changing social situations.

- *A narrow range of interests or behaviors.* DSM-5 specifies that at least two of the following symptoms must be met to qualify in this category:

  o *Repetitive, stereotyped movements or behaviors,* such as rocking, flapping, lining up toys, repetitive speech, or echoing back what was just said.

  o *Inflexible need for sameness or routine.* For example, switching the order of lunch and recess might unravel the child with ASD.

  o *Unusually deep fascination with objects or information,* such as knowing all of the details about airplanes in WWII, or always carrying around a spoon.

  o *Increased or decreased sensitivity to sensory stimuli,* such as the excessive desire for crashing into objects or watching wheels turn; or the excessive avoidance of many flavors or of tight-fitting clothes.

(APA 2013)

When a person has the above difficulties understanding the "big picture" of communicating and socializing, other symptoms often arise, such as a rigid adherence to sameness, a relative preference for mechanical things (which are predictable) rather than for people, a holding back from peers, anxiety, and very frequently associated ADHD (Kutscher 2014).

Are we beginning to see why kids with ASD might be so attracted to digital media and communication?

- On the Internet, you have the opportunity to find a multitude of similar people with similar interests.

- On the Internet, you can keep finding new information about your specific areas of interest. The Internet never ends.

- On the Internet, you can keep replaying favorite activities, such as watching the same video over, and over, and over.

- On the Internet, there are no facial expressions or body language to interpret. There is just the text to deal with.

- On the Internet, there is plenty of time to formulate your response. The speed of rapid-fire real-life peer communication—which is often happening too quickly to follow for the person with ASD—is no longer a problem.

- On the Internet, you have the opportunity to re-invent yourself—something perhaps appealing to people with ASD, who may have earned the reputation of being "odd."

- On the Internet, you can avoid participating in the real world. This might lead to a lack of practice of just the kind of social skills people on the autism spectrum need in real life. Conversely, though, communication via digital media may be an easier and thus more attractive way to "test the waters" of social communication.

- The majority of children with ASD also have co-occurring ADHD, which comes with all of its own risk factors for excessive Internet use.

Let's take a look at some of the research in the area. Studies have found that watching TV and computer use were higher in ASD adolescents, even when compared to other teens with speech/ language or learning disabilities. In particular, on any given day, 78% of ASD adolescents watched TV for approximately 2 hours/day, and 98% used computers for approximately 5 hours/day. How was that computer time spent? Answer: Overwhelmingly on websites (2.5 hours/day) and video games (2.4 hours/day). Roughly half of the ASD teens said that, on any given day, they averaged 1 hour/day of computer time on homework. Use of social networking programs, instant messaging programs, and chat rooms also occupied about 1 hour/day, but were only typically used by about 20% of ASD teens (Kuo *et al.* 2014).

Kuo and colleagues also provided the following information:

- *What did ASD teens watch on TV?* Possibly only slightly surprisingly, cartoons were the most popular TV genre, endorsed by 37% of ASD teens. Why cartoons? Perhaps, it is because they are typically targeted towards a younger audience, with less coarse and suggestive language, and are easier to understand. In second place were comedies at 15%. ASD teens who watched TV with their parents reported better relationships with their parents. Cause and effect, yet again, remain unclear. However, this invokes the American Academy of Pediatrics' recommendation, which we have already seen, that parents should co-watch the media that their children use. This is not just a safety issue, but gives parents knowledge about their child's interests, and provides concrete topics to practice conversation. Parents are particularly important in counteracting violence on the screen.

- *What type of video games did they play?* Action games, including shooting and killing games, led the field at 48%. People on the spectrum have been shown to excel in visual search tasks, have an unusual ability to note details, and have the ability to pick out small stimuli from the more general environment. These skills might lead to success in action games, and thus their appeal to ASD kids. As we have seen, violent video games have been associated with aggressive tendencies in typical teens. Thus, we need to be concerned about such a possible association with ASD teens as well. Simulation and role-playing games were the second most popular category for ASD adolescents, and accounted for 10–20% of video gaming.

- *What type of websites did they visit?* Not surprisingly, given their deep interest in factual materials, the majority of the websites they visited pertained to information and research, with information about video games being the most popular topic, and information about anime (Japanese animations) as the second most researched topic. Those teens with more severe ASD were more likely to watch news programs than those more mildly on the spectrum—perhaps because of the more straightforward nature of news programs. (Or, perhaps, they were just imitating what their parents watched.) ASD teens who used social networking programs and email from friends reported that they found social relationships more secure and positive than those who didn't. Importantly, typical teens who communicate via digital technology with family members and real-life friends also develop better social relationships than teens who spend their digital time with strangers or mere acquaintances. This appears to be due to the greater social support given by family and real friends. Once again, however, we can't distinguish cause vs. effect.

(Kuo *et al.* 2014)

How does all of this compare to typically developing siblings? Researchers (Macmullin, Lunsky and Weiss 2015; Mazurek and Weinstrup 2013) found that boys and girls on the autism spectrum both played video games for an hour more per day, and were at an increased risk for problematic video game use, than their typical siblings. Compared to those not on the spectrum, boys with ASD were more upset when not playing video games, got angrier when disturbed, and had more trouble stopping play, even though they played longer than did typical peers. More hours spent on video games, along with access to a computer or TV in the room, were factors associated with reduced sleep. Thus, ASD children with sleep problems should be assessed regarding their media habits as a point of potential therapeutic intervention.

Although people with ASD may use social media less than typical people, it does seem that when they do communicate, they prefer communicating via computer-mediated methods rather than by face-to-face interactions. A survey of 291 people with ASD and 311 people without ASD confirmed that people with ASD preferred computer-mediated interaction over face-to-face interaction as it was easier to understand and control. In addition, it helped them to express their true selves and meet similar people. Those without ASD preferred social media to maintain relationships with family and friends, as well as to meet others (Gillespie-Lynch *et al.* 2014).

Chapter 4

THE PARENTAL ROLE

In this chapter, we transition from the previous chapters, which focused primarily on the *problems* associated with media use, to the *prevention and treatment* of those problems. In other words, we'll switch from *why* it matters that our children have a balanced use of screen time, to *how* we actually achieve that balance. We'll take a look now at the parental role as both a part of the problem and a part of the solution.

What kind of role model am I for my child?

Like it or not, for better or worse, we are role models for our children. This is especially true for the younger set, where "a parent's focus of attention—whether it is cookies or computer screens or books—becomes the infants' object of desire" (Steiner-Adair and Barker 2013, p.72). Even for teens, for whom peer relations start to take over as primary drivers of behavior, their lives are affected by how we have taught and modeled appropriate behavior—and how we continue to do so.

So, we need to examine our own behavior regarding digital technology. Perhaps it would help if we look at ourselves through the eyes of our children:

- *"Dad says he needs to be available during meal times."* Do we answer the phone or check texts or emails during our family meals? Do we claim that checking that text really can't wait 20 minutes? How can we expect our children to put away their cell phones during meals when we model that we can't tolerate the delay ourselves?

- *"In fact, no matter what we're doing together, Dad stops immediately to answer his cell!"* Do we interrupt our interactions with our children whenever we receive a text, email, or phone call? What does it teach our little ones when we stop our discussions with them to have an interaction with anyone else? When anyone else in this planet of billions of people gets a higher priority than our child, what does it do to their sense of importance? Maybe we should keep our own behavior in mind when we feel insulted because our kids pause their conversation with us to check the latest text.

- *"My parents never show any interest in my games or videos."* Have we been so fixated on our own screens that we never tune in to what interests our children? That's a shame. Our participation in their digital world lets them know that we care about things that are important to them, even if we don't personally find those things to be important. Also, co-viewing or playing games with our child may actually be fun, gives us time together, and gives us an opportunity to enter their world. It allows us to teach them to examine their own thoughts and to help them understand why the media is so hard to resist. Plus, it's clear that educational media is much more effective when a child views it with a parent: "Advances in technology are not pointing to a day in which young children can simply plug in and learn without us. On the contrary, we parents are more necessary than ever" (Guernsey 2012, p.276).

- *"I guess that I never stopped to realize how much time my parents were on their own screens."* How much time do we adults spend on digital media? If parents are constantly on the computer or have the television on, won't their children see that as the norm of human behavior? Who else do they learn from? What other behaviors have they seen?

- *"If my parents have the TV on in the background all of the time—whether they are actively watching it or not—why can't I have my own digital distractions constantly running?"* This is a particularly important question since the almost constant use of TV in the house is widespread. A survey of 1000 families who were randomly selected showed that almost 40% acknowledged having the TV on most or all of the time (Guernsey 2012). The effects of background TV use on the child have been discussed in Chapter 3. Guernsey (2012) points out that moderation is the key. Fortunately, a few hours per week isn't comparable to having the TV on all the time. *So, just turn the TV off when the show you intended to watch is over.* It might help to record the programs that you really want to watch, rather than leaving the TV tuned to dribble while waiting for the good stuff. If it's too much trouble to record your "favorite" shows, what does that say about how important they are to you? Teach this technique to your children via explicit instruction and by setting an example.

- *"For as long as I can remember, my parents have always put a TV in my room. NOW they expect me to give up free access to digital media?"* A 2006 survey found that 1 in 3 children aged 0–6 years had a TV in their room. Even 1 in 5 infants less than 1 year old had a TV in their room. Why? Parental viewing behavior, again. For more than half the time, in order to watch their own shows designed for adults, the answer was to put an additional TV in the child's room (Guernsey 2012).

- *"My parents would go ballistic if I told them what I was doing on the Net, or if I were having problems."* Have we been demonstrating openness and calmness with our children?

Do they know that we may express disappointment in some of their behaviors on the Internet or otherwise, but that it's always safe for them to confide in us, and that we will always try to be a part of the solution, not a part of the problem? Are we able to convert our kids' terrible mistakes into teachable moments? Are our children confident that we will neither over-react nor become too "preachy"? Such confidence needs to be earned via constant practice of self-control on our part. It is best to start while our children are young, since by the time they are older, they will have even more challenging behaviors or experiences that will increasingly test our ability to stay rational. Indeed, we just spent the first few chapters of this book enumerating the crevices our children can fall into just through media. The consequences of their actions (bad grades, humiliation by peers, being grounded, loss of privileges, etc.) speak for themselves. We can skip the nasty attitude. Our children must know that we will heed the advice *"Watch what you say! Don't add to the drama. Practice, practice, practice"* (Steiner-Adair and Barker 2013, p.259).

We may not like what we find when we examine our own media habits and behaviors. Are we willing to limit our TV or computer use? Are we willing to shut off the TV except for those shows we really want to see? Do we like having our shortcomings or other problems being brought to attention? Do we think it would be hard to change? That it isn't worth the effort? That things are fine just as they are? That these rules apply to others but not to us? Do we think, "That could never happen to us or our child"? Do we think that our behaviors are acceptable because everyone else lives that way? Perhaps if we keep our own reactions to these issues in mind, we'll better understand the difficulties that our children will have making changes. This empathy will help us keep patient as we work with our kids, and also help us understand why the best solution is to model and enforce appropriate behaviors, starting when the children are young.

How do I set limits for my child?

Our youngsters' brains are far from fully "cooked." It takes several decades for their executive functions (a fancy psychological term for "wisdom") to gradually kick in. Meanwhile, we need to provide external limits, while simultaneously helping them develop their own self-control. Since complete elimination of technology is neither possible nor productive, our kids must rather be taught how to balance technology with the rest of their life. We need to set limits and clear expectations if the child is to develop such a well-rounded existence.

Use technology to help limit technology

Timers are a child's best friend. Yes, I know there is an app for that on their smartphone, but using the app means that the child has access to digital technology while trying to work—a mouth-watering invitation to inefficiency. A dedicated timer, however, is free of distractions. Try to create a positive attitude towards the timer. It is not to be used for punishment; rather, to announce that it is time to move on to the next activity. "Why can't they just use their watch?" you may ask. Because most kids these days don't wear a watch, if they even know where it is. They tell time with—you guessed it—their smartphone, which should have been out of the way during homework time.

Virtually all digital screen activities have ratings (follow them—your child is nothing special in that regard) or parental controls that limit content and time. User controls regarding age limits and safe searches can be set on sites such as YouTube, Netflix, and modern TVs. Use them. Find excellent advice on parental controls at www.commonsensemedia.org, www.familysafemedia.com or *The Smart Girls Guide to Internet Privacy* by V. Blue. See the Resources section at the end of this book.

Of course, parental controls don't work when our children visit a peer's house or head off to college. The best we can do is model and teach skills when they are young, and hope these skills become internalized and stick—and stay calm when they don't. That also means helping our children learn time-management skills, and how to exert voluntary attention in order to stay on task and on schedule.

Help the child develop voluntary attention control

- *Handle their requests to start media time with "'Yes, but after _____' instead of 'No'"* (Palladino 2015, p.103). The goal is for this rule to be eventually incorporated into the child's own mindset: first we deal with our responsibilities, and then there will be time for fun. "Yes, but after _____" makes it easier to exert the self-control required to delay gratification. It emphasizes that they *will* get to their preferred activity—just hold on a little bit longer. Additionally, it keeps the parent from being the "bad guy," since it places you on the "yes" side of the request.

- *Teach your child to avoid the difficult challenge of switching from an appealing activity to a non-appealing one.* Switching from a video game to homework is much, much harder than switching from homework to a video game. The former means overcoming the brain's preferential and effortless attention to sensory stimuli. Using the terminology of Chapter 1, it is easier for the brain to switch *from* tasks requiring voluntary attention (the ones that require conscious expenditure of energy to perform) *to* tasks that effortlessly grab our sensory/involuntary attention (tasks that are innately appealing such as video games) than vice-versa. Note that if someone resists getting started, the task probably requires voluntary attention. If they resist stopping, the task probably involves involuntary attention (Palladino 2015).

- *If your child had a tough time stopping the video game yesterday, don't be surprised if today doesn't go so well, either.*

THE PARENTAL ROLE

If the parent understands the physiological reasons for the difficulty getting off the video game—and expects it—they will be better able to demonstrate calm coping skills during moments of frustration. This is because frustration comes when expectations are not met. If we don't expect an easy time getting kids off the video game, then we are less likely to be frustrated or to take the resistance personally. We just happen to be the adult in the room, helping the child develop self-control. It's nothing personal. Your child is not disrespectful or bad. Rather, any attempts to be rational and exert self-control are falling prey to an over-stimulated and dopamine-intoxicated brain that is under the influence of an overwhelmingly rewarding evolutionary attraction to stimuli.

- *In any case, stay calm and guide your child to seek win–win solutions to the problem.* If you and/or your child are too overwhelmed to discuss apologies and/or solutions at the moment, everyone should take a break. Allow clear thinking to return before attempting any further interactions. The dopamine released by too much stress reduces the brain's ability to be logical. Ideally, your child can learn to recognize that they are over-stressed, and be able to call for a brief (10–15 minutes?) chill-out time. When no longer stressed, teach your child (and yourself?) how to calmly negotiate a win–win solution to the problem, before it predictably recurs. See *The Explosive Child* by R. Greene for details on this valuable approach.

- *One possible win–win solution to difficulties with transitioning off the screen is to discuss, in advance, alternative activities to which the child can transition.* Teach them the principle: if we want to avoid an activity, have alternatives readily available. During a calm moment, ask them to consider, "What am I *not* doing?" (Palladino 2015, p.100). Brainstorm together to come up with several non-media-related activities that your child could enjoy instead. Play outside. Play sports. Play an instrument. Draw. Write a poem. Volunteer. Join a club...

- *Teach your child that their escape into the media world may provide temporary pleasure, but does not solve any real-world problems.* In fact, excessive media time can exacerbate their real-life issues, sometimes even leading to an addiction cycle. See Chapter 6 on the Internet addiction spiral.

Set explicit time rules in advance

We can ease difficulties in limiting the amount of screen time by setting up explicit rules in advance of them being required. These rules at first provide external scaffolding to help the child compensate for their relative lack of self-control; but one hopes that with practice and brain growth, they will become internalized methods of controlling behavior. These rules can be set up during a family meeting, and documented in an agreement, as described in Chapter 5. Here are some examples:

- *Avoid "multi-tasking."* Some of the biggest areas of dispute revolve around the use of media while trying to do homework. Explain that "multi-tasking" is really just inefficient "multi-switching," which actually makes homework take longer since the person needs to re-orient themselves after each interruption (see Chapter 1). Thus, the family unit can agree on one of the following possible alternative ways of partitioning time. (Remember, choosing one of these alternatives is determined by what works for the child, not necessarily what would work for the parent. Your child is not just a mini-you.)

  o Do all of the homework, then do all of all of the social networking, then do all of the emails.

- ○ Work for 50 minutes and then take a 10-minute electronic devices break.

- ○ Work for 10–15 minutes and then take a 1–2-minute break.

- *Set time and location rules.* In the upcoming agreement to be negotiated with your child, we'll see that other issues to be negotiated include:

  - ○ Total amount of screen time allowed per week/ weekend night. The American Academy of Pediatrics (AAP 2013) has previously suggested 1–2 hours/ night of non-school/work-related use of electronic devices.

  - ○ Amount of time, if any, allowed to use electronic devices before starting homework.

  - ○ Location of the phone during homework, during meals, and during the night. Note that the American Academy of Pediatrics (AAP 2013) also suggests keeping TVs and Internet devices out of the child's bedroom. If your child says they can't put their cell in a central location such as the kitchen at night because they need it in their room to wake them up, get them an alarm clock.

  - ○ Turning off all incoming alerts on the cell and computer during distraction-free times.

  - ○ Use out of the house, such as while a passenger in the car, or while in waiting rooms, restaurants, etc. Allowing use during these times may make life easier—and certainly quieter—but makes exerting control later more difficult, contributes to a lack of needed down-time, and interferes with the times when many young people open up about important issues. It's during quiet times that we may hear from the back seat of the car, "Mom, did you ever smoke pot?" Burley Hofmann (2014) suggests leaving electronic devices at home. That way, there's nothing to argue about regarding their use. They are not there.

○ Use of music while doing homework. Some people find this is actually helpful in learning, making it more fun, and perhaps functioning as white noise to filter out household sounds.

○ Screen time before sleep. If there are problems getting to sleep, there should be no screen time for 1 hour before bedtime.

○ School rules. There is to be no gaming/surfing/communicating with electronic devices during class. Parents and teachers need to know that such activity is *rampant* and interferes with learning. Schools that allow open electronic devices during class time need to understand this reality. Even if Internet access is turned off or limited by the school's router, the student has their own smartphone connection to the web and has offline games loaded up. The only way the latter can be detected would be if the teacher could check live screen shots of each student from the front of the room. Not only would such a system need to be set up, it would have to be used. Trust the students if you must, but verify.

○ Cell phone use while driving. No!

○ Consequences for failure to comply. Determine what the consequences will be for breaking previously set rules. Apply these consequences without a negative attitude, which does nothing but breed further resentment.

You may need to hire an organizational coach to help organize a child's life in general. Or, you can start with the book *Organizing the Disorganized Child* (Kutscher and Moran 2009), which also covers reading, writing, and study skills. If you can't peacefully come to a family agreement, or if family dynamics are out of whack, you may need to enlist the aid of a therapist.

All pigs are created equal, but some pigs are ready for more equality than others

This commonly used expression can be adapted here to: "All pigs are created equal, but some pigs have earned and are ready for more equality than others." All family members should understand that they should adhere equally to basic philosophies such as kindness and respect on the Internet as well as in real life. This also includes not using the Internet to the point that it causes problems in life, and not engaging in activities that they are not prepared to handle. In this sense, all pigs are created equal.

However, some pigs have become more equal than others. That is to say, the same rules do not always apply to everyone equally all of the time. Adults may be equipped to watch movies with sexual content that tweens may not. Young children may not be prepared for their own cell phone. Teens who have demonstrated that they reliably get themselves off the Internet may have earned more leeway in its use. Indeed, each family member has its own developmental stage and personal history. Fair is when each person's needs (including safety) and responsibilities are met, not necessarily when all members of the family are treated identically.

Parents need to remember that they are still role models, and make sure that any exceptions they keep for themselves—such as leaving the TV on all evening or taking phone calls during dinner—are truly not setting a good example. We want to be part of the solution as good role models, not part of the problem.

Another adult responsibility: Teach how to evaluate information on the web

We think that our kids are so adept with technology that they automatically know how to critically evaluate it. Not necessarily true. A study of more than 100 undergraduate college students revealed that none of them ever checked the credentials of a website's authors (Thompson 2014). In another study, more than 1 in 3 young adults at college didn't know that search engines may include paid-for links (Thompson 2014). Website rankings are often subject to all sorts of manipulation, and search engine rankings are not a seal of a site's credentials. Anyone, with any motive, can post anything to the web, without being vetted by a publisher, peer review, teacher or librarian. Research on the web does not stop at Wikipedia; indeed, not everything on Wikipedia is correct. Some schools are beginning to teach the need for such critical evaluations of sources. Until that happens reliably at school, it is up to us to teach our children. It wouldn't hurt if we used such critical skills ourselves.

The following techniques for website evaluation are adapted from the University of Illinois Library:

- Who or what referred you to the site?

    - Did a teacher or other scholarly source refer to it? For example, was it cited by or linked from another reliable site or a library database? These sources may be more reliable than simply doing a Google search.

    - Who links to the site? Enter "link: [insert URL starting with www]" into the search bar of several search engines. You may need to shorten the URL if you get no results.

    - Ask a librarian! They are there to help you efficiently find accurate information.

- Who wrote the information?

- ○ What are the author's credentials? Are the credentials even listed? Is there contact information?

- ○ Is the author associated with an appropriate organization? (Be aware that many sites use names that sound much more official than they are.)

- ○ Do an Internet search on the author and/or the sponsoring organization.

- What is the site's purpose?

  - ○ What does the domain name tell you about the site's purpose?

    - .com is simply a personal, business or commercial site.

    - .edu sites are associated with institutes of higher education.

    - .org sites are for advocacy groups such as non-government organizations.

    - .gov is a federal website.

  - ○ Is the site trying to sell something? Look at the associated ads.

  - ○ Is the site objective, or does it have a bias?

- How accurate is the information?

  - ○ Are sources given? Is there a bibliography?

  - ○ How does this information compare to what you've found in other sources?

  - ○ Is the information up-to-date. When was it last updated? Are the links it contains functional and current?

(University of Illinois Library 2016)

That's enough to get started. It's good practice for critical thinking skills and we should be applying it to all of the information that comes our way.

The next parental role is to actually set up specific rules to deal with technology use. This involves a family meeting and a subsequent agreement, and is discussed in Chapter 5.

SETTING UP THE RULES
THE FAMILY MEETING AND AGREEMENT

Now for the nitty-gritty of actually setting up the rules regarding privileges and limits of digital technology use, in order to deal with all of the issues we've been discussing. This involves meeting with the children, and arriving at a signed agreement—one that will last until (a) it no longer works, (b) it needs alteration because of a child's developmental stage or behavior, or (c) new technology comes along. Thus, although some principles remain constant, we're chasing moving targets and will need to constantly monitor the need for change.

The family meeting

How do we know what our kids are doing? How do they know what we want them to do? How do we reach an agreement? Burley Hofmann (2014) suggests that we do our groundwork and then we talk. Although I refer to it as a family meeting, the negotiable parts are perhaps best done individually with each child.

Considerations before the family meeting

- Determine what you are worried about.
  - What is going wrong, or could go wrong, with each child?

- ○ Are you worried about the content of what they are consuming? The amount of time they are spending online? Privacy? Safety? Missing out on "real life"?

- ○ Are you worried about the psychological/learning effects, the neurological effects, or the physical effects?

- ○ Are you worried that you don't know what you don't know?

- Determine the strengths and weakness of each of your offspring.

  - ○ Look for associated conditions such as ADHD, ASD, learning disorders, anxiety, etc.

- Reach a consensus with other adults who are also responsible for your child.

- The family meeting is a time to improve family cohesiveness.

  - ○ Never come in anger.

  - ○ Stay calm.

  - ○ It is a time to come to an agreement, not a forum for discipline.

- Set the meeting's agenda:

  - ○ To help everyone choose and use technology carefully.

  - ○ To schedule time slots, total daily screen-time allowances and media choices in advance.

  - ○ To set allowable location of screens at different times of the day and night.

  - ○ To make a list of alternative activities to media consumption.

- ○ To address fairness issues for everyone.

- ○ To develop consequences of failure to comply. The goal is for family members to take responsibility for their mistakes and learn from them. Be sure that consequences are fair, and that you have the willingness to carry them out.

- ○ To seek a solution where everyone feels that their needs are met.

- ○ To discuss changes that need to be made.

- • Fortify the discussion with facts and independent recommendations. This book is full of studies and expert opinions to ground the discussion with facts rather than personal feelings.

The agreement

The previous chapters, along with the practical solutions and suggestions just listed, have prepared you for the family meeting. Let the following model agreement serve as your guide for the meeting, and as a record of your agreement. Note that some of the issues are not negotiable, whereas other issues can be addressed with a win–win attitude. You may need to negotiate and sign separate agreements with each child. Thanks go to Burley Hofmann (2014) for her wonderful sample contract upon which the following was inspired with significant modifications.

A printable version of this agreement form is available for download at www.jkp.com/catalogue/book/9781785927126.

Good luck!

SCREEN-TIME AGREEMENT

Please remember that all of the electronic devices that you use are owned by us, and the privilege of their use depends on your compliance with the rules below. Privileges are earned by establishing truthful, trustworthy, and responsible actions.

Non-negotiable rules

- You are a kind person. Being on an electronic device doesn't change that. So, treat others on the Internet the same way you would want to be treated. No cruelty, no bullying.

- You are wonderful just as you are. So, do not re-invent yourself while social-networking. You don't have time to maintain both a real-life and an onscreen personality.

- Do not post any text or picture that you wouldn't show your grandmother.

- Remember that there is no such thing as privacy or the ability to delete something once you push the "send" button. Have you heard of screen shots and forward buttons? Once it's in cyberspace, it's out there forever, incontestable proof of your actions, for all of your peers and future employers to see and pass on.

- Do not live your life on the phone. You do not need to document your entire life in photos. Important conversations should take place face-to-face.

- In case we are not brave enough to bring up subjects such as sex and drugs, we want you to raise them. No porn—it is fantasy that misrepresents and cheapens caring and compassionate relationships. We don't want you to get your information about these important topics from any bozo with the ability to upload to the Internet.

- Seek the advice of an adult if needed. We promise—or at least promise to try—to stay calm and help you.

- We will have ALL of your user names and passwords to ALL of your accounts. We reserve the right to install parental controls and site blockers, and must approve all downloads/purchases BEFORE they are accessed.

- No texting or cell phone use while driving. Turn the phone off. It can wait. People can die.

- Obey all school rules regarding smartphones and other technology.

Privileges to be negotiated (regarding times and places of use)

- Turn off the cell during family meals: yes/no.

- Allowed to use electronic devices before starting homework: yes/no. If yes, for how long? _____ minutes.

- All computers and devices with Internet connections must be used in a central location: yes/no.

- "Multi-tasking" actually makes homework take longer since you have to re-orient yourself after each interruption. To address this issue, you will (check one):

  ☐ Divide your day into time slots to first do all homework, then social media, then email.

  ☐ Take a 10-minute media break for every 50 minutes of work.

  ☐ Take a 1–2-minute break after every 10–15 minutes of work.

  ☐ Other: _____

- During homework time, you will keep your cell phone in a central location: yes/no.

- During homework time, you will turn off all incoming notifications: yes/no.

- During homework time, you can listen to music (using a radio avoids the temptations of using a smartphone): yes/no.

- Maximum screen-time/day doing non-schoolwork:

  _____

  Specify if different for weekends/vacation days:

  _____

- Time that electronics are put away on weekday nights: _____ pm/other_____

  Specify if different for weekends/vacation days:

  _____

- At bedtime, the cell phone will (check one):

  ☐ Remain in the bedroom.

  ☐ Be placed in a central location for the night.

- Media devices allowed out of the house: yes/no. If yes, where?

  _____

- If my cell phone breaks or is lost:

  _____

- Other:

  _____

  _____

This agreement is valid until changes are mutually agreed upon.

_____ Date: _____
(Person granted access to technology)

_____ Date: _____
(Person(s) who own the technology)

Chapter 6

INTERNET ADDICTION
THE FAR END OF INTERNET PROBLEMS
With Natalie Rosin

Internet problems cover a whole range of severity

Screen-time problems run along a spectrum of severity. At the mildest end are the problems we perceive among typical, well-functioning children/teens, such as texting multiple times in an hour or ignoring friends and family at get-togethers in favor of communicating elsewhere using their smartphone. Then, there are the kids whose screen-time activities result in moderate family discord and inefficient work, but who are still able to get good grades and participate in other activities such as sports. At the most severe end, there are those who suffer from what can be called a true Internet addiction: an inability to control one's digital/Internet behavior despite significant resultant problems such as falling grades, withdrawal from friends and activities, or significant family turmoil. These children/teens may react vociferously when a parent tries to limit their access to screen time.

So what distinguishes enthusiasm for an activity from a true addiction? The simplest answer is that healthy enthusiasm adds to life, whereas an addiction detracts from it. It's not the excessiveness time-wise of the behavior. Rather, it is (a) the individual's inability to control the behavior; and (b) this situation exists despite it having negative consequences. In other words, does the behavior cause problems that are out of a person's control (Rosenberg and Feder 2014)?

What is an addiction?

Thus, there are two criteria that are most commonly emphasized:

1. an inability to control one's behavior, despite...

2. significant resultant problems.

Some authors expand these to four criteria for an addiction:

1. *Excessive use* with loss of sense of time or neglect of basic drives.

2. *Withdrawal* when trying to stop. Symptoms might include anger, tension, or depression.

3. *Tolerance*, which denotes the need for more and more in order to achieve the same result. People with Internet addiction are in constant need of more time, better software, and better hardware.

4. *Negative repercussions* such as arguments, lying, social isolation, poor achievement, or fatigue.

(Young 2011)

Some authors expand these even further to nine possible criteria. Diagnostic criteria for accepted conditions are published by the American Psychiatric Association in *DSM-5* (APA 2013). At the time of *DSM-5*'s publication, there was not enough high-quality research to declare that "Internet Addiction" was an actual disorder in its own right. However, a closely related condition called "Internet Gaming Disorder" was included in a state of limbo among a bunch of other disorders to be further studied for possible future inclusion among the set of accepted conditions. Hence, preliminary criteria for Internet Gaming Disorder have been proposed. If we substituted the word *Internet* for the words *Internet gaming*, the proposed criteria when simplified would require meeting five out of the following nine traits in the last year:

1. Pre-occupation with Internet activities, i.e., constantly thinking about getting back on the Internet, as it becomes the dominant activity in your life.

2. Withdrawal symptoms when attempting to stop.

3. Tolerance (the continuous need to up the ante).

4. Attempts to stop are not successful.

5. Loss of interest in previously enjoyable activities.

6. Use continues despite awareness that the use is causing problems.

7. Have hidden/lied about the extent of Internet use.

8. Use of the Internet in order to escape problems including depression and anxiety.

9. Use has caused or significantly harmed something important, such as a relationship or job.

Such a set of criteria is still awaiting "official" validation, but it helps us to understand the kinds of difficulties associated with an Internet addiction. Recognize that *time* spent on media is not in itself a diagnostic criterion of an addiction, although some have suggested that 6–13 hours/day of non-school/work-related use is certainly most worrisome.

Note that even the name(s) of the disorder(s) is not settled yet. Authors and researchers have coined names such as:

• Internet Addiction

• Internet Gaming Addiction

• Internet Use Disorder

• iDisorder (coined by Rosen 2012)

• Problematic Internet Use

• Problematic Screen Time.

No single name can be both general enough (to cover all of the issues) *and* specific enough (to cover only the issues) to be discussed. For example, many texts refer to "Internet Addiction" but are not limiting their topic solely to online Internet activities, but also include offline gaming. Additionally, the texts may be referring to problems less severe than a full addiction. We prefer the name "Problematic Screen Time," which emphasizes that it is digital technology that is the issue, whether or not it is delivered via the Internet. The Internet Addiction Test (Young 2016) is a 20-question validated test that measures where an adult is placed along the spectrum of Internet addiction, from none to mild to moderate to severe. The test is available without charge at http://netaddiction.com/internet-addiction-test.

It also helps to clarify our thinking if we break down the term "Internet Addiction" into two types:

- *Specific addictions*—those activities that the user would have found another way to do if the Internet wasn't available. These specific addictions existed well before the Internet came into existence. Specific addictions include:

  ◦ gaming

  ◦ gambling

  ◦ pornography.

  Although the Internet has made access easier, the Internet didn't invent these types of addiction, nor does it hold a monopoly on them.

- *General addictions*—where the addiction is to the actual process of surfing the web itself, rather than to any specific content.

How does someone get addicted?
The psychological basis of addiction

How does the addiction spiral start? It can begin either with seeking enjoyment ("This game is fun!") or seeking escape ("This game takes my mind off of my grades"). In either case, the screen time leads to a pleasurable experience mediated by the neurotransmitter dopamine. Seeking repeated use is further fueled by the physiological processes of tolerance (the need for ever-stronger stimuli to produce the same effect) and withdrawal (the discomfort stemming from attempted abstinence). This constant seeking of stimuli leads to more problems in life. This starts the cycle all over again, in a downward addiction spiral of negative consequences, which becomes increasingly beyond the person's ability to control. Unfortunately, many people with ADHD are already prone to the need for rapid and immediate stimuli—which helps to explain their increased risk for all sorts of addictions.

The biological basis of addiction

Feel free to skip this section and its fancy medical terms, if you want. All we really want you to get out of it is that addiction is a physical condition that has a neurological basis for the victim spiraling down an ever-deepening, physiological black hole. An addiction is biological and frequently genetic. Thus, addicts typically need more support than simply being told, "Pull your life together!"

The biology starts with a rewarding activity such as surfing the web or playing video games. This rewarding activity activates dopamine neurons in the ventral tegmental area of the brain, which then activate the nucleus accumbens, which is the brain's pleasure/reward center. This creates the brain's sensation of a "high." Further, repeated exposure to the substrates of abuse activates glutaminergic projections to the prefrontal cortex. This increasingly forges actual neurological pathways that lead to a person's ongoing, relentless, and deepening yearnings. These neurological pathways persist long after the brain's executive function centers should have otherwise seen that the costs of the behavior outweigh the benefits (Rosenberg and Feder 2014).

Multiple MRI studies have shown differences between the brains of Internet addicts and non-addicts (Young 2015). One study found gray matter and white matter differences in areas of the brain felt to be responsible for emotional regulation and inhibition of behavior (Lin *et al.* 2014). Once again, it is not clear whether these changes are the cause or the result of the Internet behaviors, but in any case they testify to the biological underpinnings of addiction.

How common is Internet addiction?

Estimates of the prevalence of Internet addiction vary widely, based on the criteria used and country being studied, but the following rates appear to be reasonable estimates (Young 2011).

- adolescents: 4.6–4.7%

- college students: 13–18.4%

- general population: 6–15%

- ADHD: up to 25%.

(Weiss *et al.* 2011)

That's a lot of people, and the numbers refer just to the most severe end of the problematic screen-time spectrum: Internet addiction. Note that college students and people with ADHD have much higher rates than other populations.

Why is digital media so addictive?

There are myriad factors that contribute to the addictive nature of digital media.

Ready access

- Unless limits are set, digital technology is available (either online or offline) 24/7, 365 days/year.

- Parents find it convenient to allow a TV in their child's room.

- Even parents who would never consider a TV allow a computer for homework in the child's bedroom, with subsequent access to online and offline activities.

- Smartphones (which are actually mini-computers) are so small that they can be brought anywhere.

- Smartphones are so big that they don't fit well into pockets, so they are held in the hand and are thus always visible and tempting.

- Smartphones are so useful and ubiquitous that many young people find them "invisible," and are not aware of their level of dependence on them.

- Smartphones allow direct and silent access. There is no need to worry about a peer's parents questioning why the phone is ringing at midnight.

- Smartphones allow—and thus seem to demand—constant access from/to peers or workmates.

- "On-demand" services allow ready access to material at any time. Previously, broadcast TV spaced the shows out to one episode/week. Self-control was not required. Now, unlimited or "binge" watching is possible via "on-demand" technology such as Netflix, Hulu, YouTube, etc.

Digital technology is fascinating

- The machines, programs, and apps are just plain beautiful, technological marvels.

- The Internet is endless. There is no web page saying, "You've reached the end of the Internet."

- Games are often endless.

- There's something for everyone.

- The multi-media experience engages multiple senses— including our brain's natural attraction to moving images.

Digital technology meets psychological needs, especially those of teens

Steiner-Adair and Barker (2013) point out the following:

- Technology fits the needs of teens to assert their independence, as typically, much of it is done without adult supervision.

- Technology allows for the creation of "malleable identities." People can re-invent themselves on the web.

- Technology allows for the quick expression of sexual drives (but does not foster real-life intimate knowledge and caring for others, nor benefit from parental supervision).

- Technology allows for "teen drama" to play out around the clock.

- Technology allows for a quick escape from problems or a quick burst of entertainment—both leading factors of entering the addiction spiral.

What are particularly addictive Internet activities?

Not all Internet activities are equally addictive. For example:

- Time spent communicating with real friends/family (as opposed to virtual online friends) does not usually lead to addiction.

- Surfing the web for information tends to be less addictive than other online activities.

- Interactive activities that occur in real time (such as chat rooms and interactive games) may be more problematic than activities (such as email) that do not expect instantaneous, real-time interaction.

- Multi-sensory activities that contain sound and/or video are more compelling.

- Massively Multiplayer Online Role Playing Games (MMORPG) are particularly addictive. In addition to great graphics and dopamine-boosting action, these online games may involve thousands of people playing simultaneously. In real time, players make social alliances and commitments, and join competitions. If you stop playing in order to come to dinner, you miss out on these things while the rest of the players continue to socialize or advance. (This contrasts with home video game consoles, which can be paused.) Since players come from all around the world, there's no time of day or night when you can't find active players. In short, there's no end to the game, no end of players, and no end of time of day to play. *Stay away from MMORPG!* Interactive games played with a few real-life friends are much less likely to lead to addiction.

What personal traits are associated with Internet addiction?

Internet addiction is associated with many psychological conditions. Although we can't necessarily demonstrate cause vs. effect (or likely even a vicious cycle of cause leading to effect leading to more cause, etc.), it is essential that these associated conditions are detected and addressed as part of any evaluation and treatment plan. It is not quite as easy as, "I've stopped over-using the Internet. I'm cured." Relapse is likely unless the underlying conditions are resolved—for example:

- ADHD.

- A characteristic of ASD and social anxiety is that people feel uncomfortable with face-to-face communication, and this places them at high risk of excessive Internet use. The electronic world gives the users time and invisibility to construct whatever persona they wish to have.

- Preference for socializing online as opposed to direct human interaction is a strong predictor for Internet addiction.

- Loneliness.

- Depression.

- Low self-esteem.

- Other addictions such as drugs.

- Family dysfunction.

- Spending more than 20 hours/week online.

- Strong reactions to parental attempts at limiting access.

How do we treat Internet addiction?
The basics

- *Prevention is the best remedy.*

  o Address the above factors associated with Internet addiction before they lead to problems with the technology. This may involve working with a therapist and/or medication. Continue to address these issues if unresolved.

  o The rules and limit-setting strategies and agreements described in Chapters 4 and 5 form the basis for preventing an Internet addiction. These strategies include site-filtering and time-control software/hardware, and encouragement of alternative, non-technological activities such as sports. If not already undertaken, they should be implemented now.

- *Recognize that total technology abstinence is neither possible nor desirable.*

  o *Computer use is a virtual necessity for modern life,* be it at school, work, or in social situations. Unlike substance abuse where total abstinence is felt to be possible and essential, total abstinence from technology is not a viable goal.

  o *Thus, the goal is moderated use of the Internet.* For example, "I will use the computer only for work, email, and online banking."

  o *Set "bottom-line" behaviors.* For example, "I will NEVER visit gambling sites," or "I'll never stay online past midnight." In other words, moderated use will still have areas of complete abstinence from "trigger" activities.

- *Remember that addiction is a disease.* The person is fighting off the grip of psychological, neuronal, biochemical, and perhaps genetic influences. Professional help is likely to be required for a true addiction.

Interventions with a therapist

Commonly suggested therapies—mediated by a professional *therapist specializing in addiction*—include motivational interviewing, Cognitive Behavioral Therapy (CBT), Dialectic Behavioral Therapy (DBT), and Family Therapy.

Motivational interviewing

Many addicts are very ambivalent about giving up their addictive activity. They may be afraid of loss of an area of socialization, of fun, or of escape from real-life problems. Indeed, they may not even be convinced that they really have a problem. The goal of motivational interviewing is to get them to recognize and overcome this ambivalence, and thus be able to change their behavior.

The process involves questions designed to elicit details about their Internet use (hours spent and sites visited in order of importance to them, etc.), how the Internet makes them feel and how it has affected their lives. Of particular help is for the person to pay attention to how they feel just before getting onto the screen-time activity (e.g., depressed about school, or work not going well, or angry over a fight with family or friends, etc.). The client is then guided to acknowledge the source and consequences of their activities, to take responsibility for them, to overcome their ambivalence, and thus to engage in helpful strategies (Young 2015).

Cognitive Behavioral Therapy

Cognitive Behavioral Therapy (CBT) is widely used for substance, depression, anxiety, Obsessive–Compulsive Disorder (OCD) and other behavioral disorders. It is guided by a therapist, and can perhaps best be started individually and then followed up with group therapy. CBT has several major components, including:

- *Functional analysis* explores the root triggers of dysfunction, and how the negative behaviors provide short-term relief/pleasure and thus powerfully reinforce the negative behaviors. Internet addicts may think that the Internet treats them better than the real world. Practitioners help clients realize that reliance on the virtual world reinforces temporary escape but doesn't solve real-world problems or lead to true self-esteem. Real life has opportunities that can satisfy real needs—with correct strategies and efforts. Thus, CBT helps the client restructure distorted thoughts. This is an example of the "cognitive" part of CBT.

- *Skills training* helps to develop useful coping skills and adaptive behaviors to replace dysfunctional ones. These skills include organization, prioritization, time management, development of satisfying alternative activities, linkage to supporting resources, and specific techniques to handle stressors. These are examples of the "behavioral" part of CBT.

Dialectic Behavioral Therapy (DBT)

DBT is a form of CBT, with emphasis on validation—that is, accepting uncomfortable thoughts, feelings and behaviors (vs. struggling with them). DBT seeks to establish a balance between acceptance and change, and thus helps the person reach the goal of gradual transformation. DBT also focuses on coping skills, relaxation techniques, and mindfulness.

Family Therapy

The family may have *contributed to* the addict's addiction; and/or, the family may have *suffered from* the addict's addiction. Probably both. There is probably room for legitimate complaints from everyone involved. Whichever case applies, therapy aims to promote the individual's recovery by repairing the damaged relationship. We need to help the family view themselves as "therapists," rather than viewing themselves as "victims." The goal of therapy, then, is to bring the family back as an essential supportive resource.

Other therapies

Other treatment approaches that have been tried include 12-Step programs based upon the principles of Alcoholics Anonymous, Mindfulness-Based Meditation, Transcendental Meditation, and yoga.

Unfortunately, well-controlled studies are hard to come by, and further research is still needed to prove the effectiveness of any one treatment over another (Weiss *et al.* 2011). Meanwhile, it seems reasonable to conclude that Internet addiction seems to be treatable, particularly with CBT (Dau, Banger and Banger 2015). The role of medications (not including those for treating associated conditions) and possible use of multiple therapies has yet to be defined.

Chapter 7

SUMMARY

I'm worried about my child's technology use. Why does my son scream when I try to get him off the computer? Is my daughter honest about her Internet activities? Just how much screen time is too much? Just how do I set limits without starting World War III? What effect is all of this technology having on my child's learning and behavior?

I summarize here what is known about the extent of our amorous behavior with our screens, along with its effects on our brains and our lives. I discuss how to successfully co-exist with the plethora of benefits and threats coming our way courtesy of digital technology. Further information and references can be found in the main text.

The recent explosion of digital technology and services

The rapid explosion of digital technology in the past 15 years has led to unprecedented opportunities and challenges for us all. Just consider the new technological *devices* since 2000: iPods, iPhones, iPads, Android, camera phones, broadband modems, Wi-Fi, HD TVs, and Roku. New technology *services* since 2000 include Facebook, Twitter, Skype, Instagram, MySpace, LinkedIn, iTunes, Netflix, Hulu, YouTube, hi-tech online games, Apps, and Firefox (Rosen 2012). That's all on top of our "old" technology such as video games, texting, email, and television. Collectively referred to as "screen time," these activities have been quite a lot to adjust to in 15 years.

There are myriad unbelievable benefits that we can derive from digital technology. It's fun, provides limitless news, intellectual thought, art, entertainment, and instant communication allowing people to work together around the globe, etc.

The extent of screen-time usage

This technology takes up a tremendous amount of our children's day (and night). According to the American Academy of Pediatrics 2013 policy statement:

- 8–10-year-old children spend nearly 8 hours/day on media.

- Older children and teens spend more than 11 hours/day on media.

- 71% of children have a TV or Internet device in their room.

- 1 in 3 teens sends more than 100 texts/day (largely replacing phone use).

- Our children spend more time with media than in school, and media use is second only to sleep as the leading activity.

- Yet, 2 out of 3 children and teens say that their parents have no media rules.

(AAP 2013)

The fascination with technology spills over into the classroom, where 62% of iGeneration (teenage) students state that they check their digital devices more frequently than every 15 minutes (Rosen 2012). It is not just children who are so hooked on their screens: 1 in 3 adults says that they check their mobile device before getting out of bed in the morning (Rosen 2012).

The parents' dilemma and role in setting limits

Parents watch their child spend hours on digital devices, and are torn between the emotions of *pride* over their prodigy's technical prowess, *happiness* that they are preparing their child for the future, and *fear* about the as yet incompletely known possible effects of all of this technology use on their child's brain and future.

Technology by itself is neither good nor bad. Rather, as we shall see, it is its usage and the limits we teach our children to put on it that determines whether technology has a good or bad effect on society.

Problems with the *use* of digital technology

According to one teacher survey (Porter 2013):

- Nearly 90% of teachers felt technology had created a distracted generation with short attention spans.

- Almost 50% felt it hurt critical thinking and homework ability.

- 76% felt students were conditioned to find quick answers.

- 60% felt it hindered writing and face-to-face communication. Communication with full sentences and longer has lost out to short snippets in writing or media.

In short, technology is changing the way our students learn, and not always for the better.

Does technology interfere with classroom work?

According to a student survey (Rosen 2012), 62% of the iGeneration check for text messages and 32% check into Facebook every 15 minutes or less! All of this activity comes at a price in learning. In one study, students who sent text messages while watching a lecture had exam scores 19% below those who did not text (Thompson 2014). Students recognize that texting in school not only interferes with their own learning, but also interferes with other students' attention—yet 49% of them still felt it was okay to text during class (Rosen 2012).

Not surprisingly, allowing web access to students during a lecture doesn't fare well, either. One group of students was allowed to surf the web during class, and the other kept their laptops closed. Students did indeed look at lecture-related sites, but also went shopping, watched videos, and caught up on email. Even those students who surfed only on topics related to the lecture showed significantly worse recall of the lecture's content than those who kept their laptops closed (Carr 2011).

Which is better? Taking notes with a pen and paper or with a laptop?

Pen and paper. Probably. There are multiple apparent reasons for pen and paper's superiority in learning. First, there are the benefits that come from the actual formation of the letters with the student's hands. Second, with a laptop, it is possible to keep pace with the lecturer and thus revert to a verbatim, passive "transcription mode," relegating any actual learning until later. With slower, handwritten notes, the student can only keep up with the lecturer by documenting the crux of the material—which involves active involvement during class. Third, keyboards are attached to distracting technology; and fourth, it is harder to move around the page using laptops. Although there is some variation in findings, current studies suggest caution in switching to keyboards for note-taking. Future technologies and strategies of future students may change the recommendations.

Does reading on a screen interfere with in-depth learning?

Yes. In a number of ways:

- Screens lack the tactile experience of the printed page.

- Hypertext is distracting and makes it harder to know where you are on the web.

- Shallow reading becomes the norm. Gone are the days of following an author's extensive, logically presented thoughts.

- Digital distractions are right there on the machine.

Screen reading is probably fine for short texts such as news articles. (The average web page holds the reader for 18 seconds.) However, most people have been found to prefer the printed page for more serious reading that will require revisiting parts of the text—such as studying. 92% of US students preferred hard copy for long schoolwork texts as well as for long texts when reading for pleasure.

There is concern that the reliance upon shallow reading may interfere with the development of deep reading skills such as thoughtful pondering, critical analysis and inferential thinking. It is feared that neurological connections required for deep reading— for example, brain areas involved in visual processing and phonological processing—may not be made in those people who learn primarily via shallow reading (Loh 2015).

How does our attention system work?

First, we need to briefly explain about the different kinds of attention. There are basically three types of attentional networks, which are continually jockeying with each other for expression:

- *Stay-on-task network.* This requires willful attention to a given job. It is the function that allows us to actually execute a plan in a linear fashion. This network is also called "voluntary attention," and is needed for tasks such as homework.

- *Sensory/emergency network.* No matter what else we are doing, our sensory network is constantly scanning our environment for emergency issues of safety or opportunity. This sensory-seeking network requires no willful energy, and is also called "involuntary attention." Like news bulletins, it breaks through any state of mind. Thus, video games that feature movement effortlessly demand our attention through the sensory/emergency network, easily pulling us off the stay-on-task network that is trying to willfully force our attention on a boring task such as writing an essay.

- *Daydreaming network.* This occurs when the other networks are not actively dealing with some other situation. It is the time when the brain ponders, thinks in a creative non-linear fashion, consolidates learning, and restores itself. It occurs during down-time, sleep, and even during reading when we pause to consider the significance of what we have just read.

Switching from one of these networks to another requires an expenditure of energy by a part of the brain called the insula.

The myth of "multi-tasking"

How does our attention system deal with "multi-tasking"? Answer: It doesn't.

There's no such thing as "multi-tasking." Rather, current thinking is that people "multi-switch" back and forth so frequently from one activity to another that they get the sensation that they are doing two things simultaneously, but they are actually only paying attention to one thing at any given moment. You can't type a text message and read your textbook at the same time!

So, let's re-word the question: How does our attention system deal with "multi-*switching*"? Answer: not so great.

Attempts to multi-switch during school work present a triple whammy. First, there is the time to actually answer/ deal with the interruption. Second, there is the tremendously wasteful expenditure of time as the child returns to where they were before the interruption. Third, their brain is further slowed down by the energy and stress expended as the insula gets whiplash endeavoring to switch from one activity to another. Keep this in mind as you make arrangements with your child about keeping distracting devices (which invite multi-switching) in their room during homework time.

Multi-switching is inefficient, and thus decreases free time. Your child will have more free time and less stress if they put away their digital technology while studying.

Constant use of screens diminishes the benefits of down-time

Screen-time activities have replaced allowing our brain to wander while commuting to work, walking between classes, or waiting for an appointment. The benefits of the daydreaming network are diminished.

Screens cut into time for unstructured play, structured play, and other activities

Screen-time activities also interfere with unstructured play. After reviewing decades of research, the American Academy of Pediatrics concluded that screenless, unstructured play provides the best avenue for young children to learn the skills of problem solving, reasoning, communication, creativity, and motor skills. Excessive media use also cuts into free time that could have been utilized for other productive activities, such as learning how to get along with real-life people, structured play with family members, sports, music, drama, etc.

ADHD kids, in particular, lose out on opportunities to practice controlling impulsivity, attention, socialization, and self-control issues. In fact, video games by their very nature may actually reinforce those negative traits. (On the flip side, though, digital technology is the currency of much of a child's socialization with peers, and may thus have a beneficial social effect as well as possibly teach certain skills such as reading.)

Screens interfere with developing voluntary attention

Voluntary attention—the ability to willfully control where to focus your attention and thus control your actions—is a critical skill to master. It is, perhaps, the most important predictor of future success. Thus, when we teach our kids to exercise the self-control (volitional attention) necessary to get off their screens, they are developing one of life's most important skills.

Areas where digital learning does excel

Of course, there are areas where digital learning is advantageous:

- eReading saves paper.

- eReading may improve access to books and other information in areas with limited resources.

- Technologies enhanced by computers are appealing to students, and seem to keep them involved in learning that requires rehearsal/repetition. Importantly, all of these technologies are more effective with teacher support (Greenfield 2015).

- Special needs students show largely positive benefits from digital technologies. This includes children with dyslexia, visual impairment, autism spectrum disorders, and intellectual disability—improving either their ability to learn or to communicate (Greenfield 2015).

Other psychological effects of the Internet

Gardner and Davis (2014) identify issues relating to identity formation, intimacy, and imagination: On the Internet, you can create whatever identity you want. Your life can be perfect online. Or, it can be hell, especially as your sense of identity may depend upon how quickly and how many "likes" you garner. Intimacy may be improved by easier communication, or hampered by superficial exchanges. Imagination can be boosted by opening doors to collaboration, or stifled by mimicry.

Association with other psychological conditions

Many studies show that excessive digital technology use is associated with a wide variety of psychological conditions. It is essential to note that for most of these associations, which is the cause and which is the effect has not been determined. Associated conditions include ADHD, ASD, anxiety, OCD, depression, school problems, relationship problems, and addictions to substances, food, sex, or gambling.

Neurological effects of Internet abuse

In summary, brain imaging studies show that, compared to the general population, people with an Internet addiction have decreased gray matter in areas of the brain that are responsible for cognitive control, inhibition of incorrect responses, execution of goal-directed behavior, motivation, and reward processing, Imaging studies also reveal white matter (the connecting highways between areas of the brain) differences in areas that control memory and multi-sensory input (Yuan *et al.* 2011). It remains unclear as to whether these changes are the cause or the result of Internet addiction.

Physical effects of digital media use

Physical effects include: poor sleep, daytime sleepiness, backaches, musculoskeletal pain, headaches, over- and under-eating, substance abuse, smoking, exposure to pornography that does not show safe sex, distracted driving injuries, distracted walking injuries, repetitive movement thumb injuries, hearing loss from earphones, hypercholesterolemia, hypertension, and asthma; and unfortunately even many deaths from toppling untethered TVs and dressers, and "death by selfies" as people put themselves into precarious situations to take a picture.

Problems with the *content* of digital technology
Social media issues

Social media is so enticing because you can re-invent (i.e., "airbrush") your life, and is so difficult because of the time it takes to keep up such an image. Further, everyone else's (secretly airbrushed) life seems so much better than yours. They seem to have more "friends" or "likes." Then, there's cyber-bullying, rampant sexting, and giving out too much information to heaven-knows-who. Studies show that almost 50% of teens have revealed to strangers personal information such as physical descriptions or photos. Although a great deal of time is spent on digital media, 2 out of 3 children and teens say that their parents have no media rules.

Does exposure to pornography and other media affect sexuality?

Yes. Unless responsible adults get involved, youth don't know that pornography is just fantasy—demeaning fantasy that typically doesn't model respect, affection, or safe-sex practices. A great deal of research clearly demonstrates a relationship between media exposure to sex (including TV, music lyrics, movies, and Internet) and earlier sexual activity. A survey of 12–17-year-old girls revealed that they felt media pressure to start having sex. Exposure to media sexual content doubles the risk of early sexual intercourse, and a TV in a child's bedroom is associated with greater sexual activity and drug use by teenagers.

Does media exposure increase the risk of violent behavior?

Yes. The answer, based on an overwhelming predominance of research, shows a definite association between violence presented digitally and aggressive, violent behavior. The evidence is close to conclusive that the media exposure actually is causative, not merely statistically associated. These conclusions were reached by an American Academy of Pediatrics (AAP 2009a) policy statement on media violence, which referenced similar conclusions by the National Institute of Mental Health (NIMH) and the Federal Communications Commission (FCC). Violence on TV has been estimated to have been viewed 200,000 times on TV by the time our children reach the age of 18 years. That exposure demonstrates using violence and guns as a way of conflict resolution. Movie violence doesn't help either. Rap, heavy metal, and rock tend to revolve around death, homicide, suicide, drug abuse, and sex. The lyrics of these music genres are often racist, homophobic, and sexually demeaning to women, and frequently glorify smoking, alcohol, and drugs. Rap and heavy metal music and music videos are associated (but not yet shown to be causal) with reckless behavior, including substance abuse and sexual promiscuity. Media consumes so much of a child's life that it is replacing parents and teachers as role models (AAP 2009a).

Do violent video games lead to violent behavior?

Yes. There is strong evidence that playing violent video games (which represent 60% of video game sales) leads to aggressive behavior. An exhaustive meta-analysis of 381 tests on over 130,000 participants found that violent video games significantly increased aggressive cognition, aggressive behavior, and physical arousal; meanwhile they decreased sensitivity to violence and positive social interaction. It is less clear, though, how long these effects last, and whether they invariably carry over into real-life scenarios. So far, no studies demonstrate a direct lead to criminal-level violence.

Does media affect substance use?

Yes. 70% of movies made in 2010 still contained smoking, without any mention of its negative effects. Studies show that exposure to movies with smoking during grades 5–8 predicts starting to smoke 1–8 years later. Similar statements can be made about alcohol use (Strasburger *et al.* 2010).

Resultant American Academy of Pediatrics recommendations regarding digital media

- Media, including TV, smartphones, music lyrics, and music videos, contribute to effects on sexuality and violence. This should be discussed with your doctor.

- Limit total entertainment screen time to less than 1–2 hours/day.

- Do not allow TV or Internet-connected devices in the child's bedroom. A TV in the child's bedroom makes it harder to monitor what they are watching, has been found to increase a child's exposure to TV by 1 hour/day, is associated with worse school performance, raises the risk of smoking by a factor of two, and the risk of obesity rises by 31%. The latter is probably related to commercials pushing poor food choices as well as the possibility of decreasing physical exercise.

- Monitor children's/teen's media and the websites they visit.

- Co-view media with your child and teen. This is for safety and also to open up discussions.

- Model good media behavior. Studies show that the heavy media use of parents is the strongest predictor of heavy media use in their children. Parental discussion of issues presented by media has been found to be successful in countering harmful content, including their children being less likely to engage in risky sexual behaviors (Strasburger *et al.* 2010).

- Set up a family plan (AAP 2013).

The American Academy of Pediatrics is in the process of updating its recommendations, placing more emphasis on content and parent/child collaboration than on specific time limits.

Problems regarding specific populations
Very young children and screen time
Statistics on usage

Despite the American Academy of Pediatrics' discouragement, 90% of children less than 2 years of age have some type of screen time (AAP 2011a). The average child under 2 years watches television for 1–2 hours/day. This does not include exposure to 4 hours or more of "background" TV, where the adult has the TV on—whether paying attention to it or not.

Is there any benefit to screen time for children less than 2 years old?

Not that we know of. Educational claims of screen-time activity for children less than 2 years old remain unproven. Even studies of 2-year-olds watching high-quality educational programs such as *Sesame Street* have found either no effect or even a negative effect. It seems that real people, who are physically present and paying attention, are most effective at engaging an infant's learning centers—especially if the infant has formed a bond with them (Steiner-Adair and Barker 2013).

What about 3–5-year-olds?

The cognitive skills of babies are in sharp contrast to those of slightly older children from ages 3–5. For this latter age group, research has shown that high-quality educational programs such as *Sesame Street, Barney, Dora the Explorer, Blue's Clues,* and *Mister Rogers* help to improve language, social skills, and school readiness, which may persist into adolescence (Guernsey 2012).

Does "background" or "second-hand" TV interfere with child development?

Heavy media usage by the family may interfere in a child's development by reducing the amount of time parents spend talking to, reading to, and playing with their children. In addition, it cuts into the child's own unstructured playtime and reading. Several studies have associated heavy TV use with language delay, especially if the child watches alone. Again, these are studies that cannot separate cause and effect.

Children with ADHD and screen time
ADHD traits that make screen time so appealing

Children with ADHD can't inhibit (block out) incoming stimuli, leading to difficulty sustaining voluntary attention on activities that are not naturally appealing. Their sensory/warning attention system keeps them glued to the movement, sounds, and challenges of digital media. Further, video games are constantly changing, they give and demand immediate feedback, and they provide frequent but not totally satisfying hits of dopamine to the brain's reward centers (with the promise of even bigger rewards if the person just gets to the next level). Other digital media problems include poor foresight and impulsivity when it comes to navigation through the minefields of the web. All of this puts people with ADHD at risk for Internet problems. Estimates of Internet addiction in the ADHD population run as high as 25%—much higher than in the control population.

Unfortunately, digital games seem to be a double whammy for people with ADHD: they reinforce the negatives (such as lack of patience and the need for immediate rewards), and diminish opportunities to develop the positives (such as sports and clubs). Note that gaming does have some positive neurological training, such as improving visual–spatial skills, and some games reinforce the ability to inhibit.

Children with ASD and screen time
ASD traits that make screen time so appealing

On the Internet, there are no facial expressions or body language to interpret, there is time to formulate your response, you can re-invent yourself as you wish, and you can find similar people. Communication via digital media may thus be an easier and more attractive way to "test the waters" of social communication. Another feature of the Internet that attracts people on the autism spectrum is the ability to keep digging deeper and deeper into areas of interest (and replay them again and again), which simultaneously allows the person to escape from the confusing pressures of the real world. Further, the majority of people with ASD also have ADHD, bringing in the issues revolving around ADHD just discussed.

The result? Research has found that watching TV and computer use were higher in ASD adolescents, even when compared to other teens with speech/language or learning disabilities. Cartoons are a particular area of interest, along with information sites such as those devoted to gaming hints and anime. Social media was used less than by neurotypicals, although people on the autism spectrum preferred communicating via computer rather than by face-to-face interactions.

The parental role
What kind of role model am I for my child?

They're watching us! Do we bring our phone to family meals? Do we interrupt our time with our kids to take a call from anyone else in the world? Do we show any interest in their online activities, both for safety and to show that we care about their interests? Do we keep the TV on even when we're not actively watching it?

Have we been demonstrating openness and calmness with our children? Do they know that we may express disappointment in some of their behaviors on the Internet or otherwise, but that it's always safe for them to confide in us?

How do I set limits for my child (until they are mature enough to limit themselves)?

Use technology to help limit technology. Pay attention to maturity/content ratings. Use parental controls on hardware and software to limit content and time. See the Resources section of this book.

Help your child develop their own voluntary attention control:

- Keep things positive by answering their request to start media time with, "Yes, but after _____" instead of "No."

- Teach that escape into the media world does not solve real-life problems.

- Stay calm, and guide your child to seek win–win solutions.

- Set explicit rules regarding time, content, and placement of devices in advance.

- Avoid multi-switching by establishing times/breaks for screen time.

Setting up the rules: The family meeting and agreement
The family meeting

It is time to all get together and calmly discuss the rules. Before the meeting, parents should determine what they are worried about, along with an evaluation of each child's strengths and weaknesses. Parents need to reach a consensus with each other before entering into discussion with their children. The meeting itself should be presented as a time to come to an agreement, not as a forum for discipline.

The agenda is to seek the time, place, and content of digital technology use in a fair, win–win fashion, along with fair consequences for failure to comply. Fortify the discussion with actual facts and independent recommendations as provided in this book.

The meeting can be guided by the "Screen-Time Agreement" found on page 92. A separate agreement may be required for each child.

Internet addiction: The far end of Internet problems
What is an addiction?

At its core, an addiction is defined as (1) an inability to control one's behavior, despite (2) significant resultant problems. Other common criteria are withdrawal when trying to stop, tolerance (which is the need for more and more in order to achieve the same results), its use as an escape, and pre-occupation with getting back to the addictive activity. Internet addiction is awaiting sufficient scientific evidence for its existence before it will be entitled to "official" recognition as a disorder by the American Psychiatric Association. Reasonable estimates of

Internet addiction prevalence appear to be 6–15% of the US general population, and 13–18.4% of college students.

The psychological basis of addiction

How does the addiction spiral start? It can begin with either seeking enjoyment ("This game is fun!") or seeking escape ("This game takes my mind off of my grades"). In either case, the screen time leads to a pleasurable experience mediated by the neurotransmitter dopamine. The seeking of repeated use is further fueled by the physiological processes of tolerance and withdrawal. This constant seeking of stimuli leads to more problems in life. This starts the cycle all over again, in a downward addiction spiral.

What are particularly addictive Internet activities?

Not all Internet activities are equally addictive. For example:

- Time spent communicating with real friends/family (as opposed to virtual online friends) does not usually lead to addiction.

- Surfing the web for information tends to be less addictive than other online activities.

- Interactive activities that occur in real time (such as chat rooms and interactive games) may be more problematic than activities that do not expect instantaneous, real-time interaction such as email.

- Massively Multiplayer Online Role Playing Games (MMORPG) are particularly addictive.

How do we treat Internet addiction?
The basics

- *Prevention is the best remedy.*

  ○ Address predisposing issues before they lead to problems with technology.

  ○ The rules and limit-setting strategies and agreements of Chapter 5 form the basis for preventing an Internet addiction.

- *Recognize that total technology abstinence is neither possible nor desirable.*

  ○ *Computer use is a virtual necessity for modern life,* be it at school, work, or in social situations. Unlike substance abuse where total abstinence is felt to be possible and essential, total abstinence from technology is not a viable goal.

  ○ *Thus, the goal is moderated use of the Internet.* For example, "I will use the computer only for work, email, and online banking."

  ○ *Set "bottom-line" behaviors.* For example, "I will NEVER visit gambling sites," or, "I'll never stay online past midnight."

Interventions with a therapist

Commonly suggested therapies—mediated by a professional therapist specializing in addiction—include motivational interviewing, Cognitive Behavioral Therapy (CBT), Dialectic Behavioral Therapy (DBT) and Family Therapy.

REFERENCES

AAP (American Academy of Pediatrics) (2009a) "Policy Statement—Media violence." *Pediatrics 124*, 3, 1495–1503.

AAP (American Academy of Pediatrics) (2009b) "Policy Statement—Impact of music, music lyrics, and music videos on children and youth." *Pediatrics 124*, 5, 1488–1494.

AAP (American Academy of Pediatrics) (2010) "Policy Statement—Sexuality, contraception, and the media." *Pediatrics 126*, 3, 576–582.

AAP (American Academy of Pediatrics) (2011a) "Council on Communications and Media: Media use by children younger than 2 years." *Pediatrics 128*, 5, 1040–1045.

AAP (American Academy of Pediatrics) (2011b) "Babies and toddlers should learn from play, not screens." Available at www2.aap.org/advocacy/releases/mediaunder2.htm, accessed on 5 November 2015.

AAP (American Academy of Pediatrics) (2013) "Children, adolescents and the media: Council on communications and media." *Pediatrics 132*, 5, 58–61.

APA (American Psychiatric Association) (2013) *Diagnostic and Statistical Manual of Mental Disorders, 5th edition (DSM-5)*. Arlington, VA: American Psychiatric Publishing.

Baron, N. (2015) *Words Onscreen: The Fate of Reading in a Digital World*. New York, NY: Oxford University Press.

Brown, A., Shifrin, D., and Hill, D. (2015) "Beyond 'turn it off': How to advise families on media use." *AAP News* (28 September, 2015).

Burley Hofmann, J. (2014) *iRules: What Every Tech-Healthy Family Needs to Know About Selfies, Sexting, Gaming, and Growing Up*. New York, NY: Rodale.

Carr, N. (2011) *What the Internet Is Doing to Our Brains: The Shallows*. New York, NY: W. W. Norton and Company.

Christakis, D. (2009) "The effects of infant media usage: What do we know and what should we learn." *Acta Paediatrica 1*, 8–16.

Dau, W., Banger, H., and Banger, M. (2015) "Therapeutic Interventions in the Treatment of Problematic Internet Use—Experiences from Germany." In C. Montag and M. Reuter (eds) *Internet Addiction: Neuroscientific Approaches and Therapeutical Interventions*. Basel, Switzerland: Springer International Publishing.

REFERENCES

Duran, L. and Frederick, C. (2016) "Information comprehension: Handwritten vs. typed notes." *Undergraduate Research Journal for the Human Sciences 12.* Available at www.kon.org/urc/v12/duran.html, accessed on 2 May 2016.

Eapen, C., Kumar, B., Bhat, A. K. and Venugopal, A. (2014) "Extensor pollicis longus injury in addition to de Quervain's with text messaging on mobile phones." *Journal of Clinical and Diagnostic Research 8,* 11, LC01–4.

Gardner, H. and Davis, K. (2014) *The App Generation: How Today's Youth Navigate Identity, Intimacy, and Imagination in a Digital World.* New Haven, CT: Yale University Press.

Gillespie-Lynch, K., Kapp, S., Shane-Simpson, C., Shane Smith, D., *et al.* (2014) "Intersections between the autism spectrum and the internet: Perceived benefits and preferred functions of computer-mediated communication." *American Association of Intellectual and Developmental Disabilities 52,* 6, 456–469.

Glatter, R. (2012) *Texting while walking?—Think twice.* Available at www.forbes.com/sites/robertglatter/2012/07/31/texting-while-walking-think-twice/#2d79261d28ab, accessed on 7 May 2016.

Greenfield, S. (2015) *Mind Change: How Digital Technologies Are Leaving Their Mark on Our Brains.* New York, NY: Random House.

Griffiths, M., Kuss, D. and Demetrovics, Z. (2014) "Social Networking Addiction." In K. Rosenberg and L. Feder (eds) *Behavioural Addictions: Criteria, Evidence, and Treatment.* London: Elsevier.

Guernsey, L. (2012) *Screen Time: How Electronic Media—From Baby Videos to Educational Software—Affects Your Young Child.* Philadelphia, PA: Basic Books.

Huang, A. (2015) "Autonomic Nervous System and Brain Circuitry for Internet Addiction." In C. Montag and M. Reuter (eds) *Internet Addiction: Neuroscientific Approaches and Therapeutical Interventions.* Basel, Switzerland: Springer.

Kennedy Krieger Institute (2015) "Adolescents need audiological screenings too." *Clinical Connection.* Available at www.kennedykrieger.org/sites/default/files/overview_file/clinical-connection-spring-summer-2015.pdf, accessed on 14 May 2016.

Kuo, M., Orsmond, G., Coster, W., and Cohn, E. (2014) "Media use among adolescents with autism spectrum disorder." *Autism 18,* 8, 914–923.

Kutscher, M. (2014) *Kids in the Syndrome Mix of ADHD, LD, Autism Spectrum, Tourette's, Anxiety and More!: The One-Stop Guide for Parents, Teachers, and Other Professionals* (2nd edn). London: Jessica Kingsley Publishers.

Kutscher, M. and Moran, M. (2009) *Organizing the Disorganized Child: Simple Strategies to Succeed in School.* New York, NY: HarperCollins Publishers.

Levitin, D. (2014) *The Organized Mind: Thinking Straight in the Age of Information Overload.* New York, NY: Plume/Penguin.

Lin, F. and Lei, H. (2015) "Structural Brain Imaging and Internet Addiction." In C. Montag and M. Reuter (eds) *Internet Addiction.* Basel, Switzerland: Springer International.

Lin, X., Dong, G., Wang, Q., and Du, X. (2014) "Abnormal gray matter and white matter volume in Internet gaming addicts." *Addictive Behaviors 40,* 137–143.

Loh, K. (2015) "How has the Internet reshaped human cognition?" *The Neuroscientist*. DOI: 10.1177/1073858415595005.

Macmullin, J., Lunsky, Y., and Weiss, J. (2015) "Plugged in: Electronics use in youth and young adults with autism spectrum disorder." *Autism*. DOI: 10.1177/1362361314566047.

Mazurek, M. and Weinstrup, C. (2013) "Television, video game and social media use among children with ASD and typically developing siblings." *Journal of Autism and Developmental Disorder 43*, 6, 1258–1271.

Mueller, P. and Oppenheimer, D. (2014) "The pen is mightier than the keyboard: The advantages of longhand over laptop note taking." *Psychological Science 25*, 6, 1159–1168.

Palladino, L. (2015) *Parenting in the Age of Attention Snatchers: A Step-by-Step Guide to Balancing Your Child's Use of Technology*. Boston, MA: Shambhala.

Porter, A. (2013) "The problem with technology in schools." *The Washington Post* (28 January 2013).

Products Safety Project (2015). Available at www.productsafetyproject. com/child-deaths-from-falling-tvs-are-all-too-common-what-can-we-do/#sthash.zseux2X7.dpuf, accessed on 2 May 2016.

Rideout, V. (2010) *Generation M2: Media in the Lives of 8- to18-year-olds*. Menlo Park, CA: Kaiser Family Foundation.

Rosen, L. (2012) *iDisorder: Understanding Our Obsession with Technology and Overcoming Its Hold on Us*. New York, NY: Palgrave Macmillan.

Rosenberg, K. and Feder, L. (2014) "An Introduction to Behavioral Addictions." In K. Rosenberg and L. Feder (eds) *Behavioural Addictions: Criteria, Evidence, and Treatment*. London: Elsevier.

Salie, F. (2016) Death by selfie. *CBS News* (March 6, 2016). Available at www. cbsnews.com/news/death-by-selfie, accessed on 2 May 2016.

Science Daily (2014) "Think it's safe to type a quick text while walking? Think again." University of Buffalo; 3 March 2014. Available at www.sciencedaily. com/releases/2014/03/140303143347.htm, accessed on 2 May 2016.

Smahel, D., Wright, M., and Cernikova, M. (2015) "The impact of digital media on health: Children's perspectives." *International Journal of Public Health 60*, 131–137.

Steiner-Adair, C. and Barker, T. (2013) *The Big Disconnect: Protecting Childhood and Family Relationships in the Digital Age*. New York, NY: HarperCollins Publishers.

Strasburger, V., Jordan, A. and Donnerstein, E. (2010) "Health effects of media on children and adolescents." *Pediatrics 125*, 756.

Suris, J. C., Akre, C., Piguet, C., Ambresin, A.-E., *et al.* (2014) "Is Internet use unhealthy? A cross-sectional study of adolescent Internet overuse." *Swiss Medical Weekly* 144:w14061.

Thompson, C. (2014) *Smarter than You Think: How Technology is Changing Our Minds for the Better*. New York, NY: Penguin Books.

University of Illinois Library (2016) *Evaluating internet sources*. Available at www. library.illinois.edu/ugl/howdoi/webeval.html, accessed on 2 May 2016.

REFERENCES

Weiss, M., Baer, S., Blake, A., Saran, K. *et al.* (2011) "The screens culture: Impact on ADHD." *ADHD Attention Deficit Hyperactivity Disorder 3*, 327–334.

White, T. (2015) "Subclinical psychiatric symptoms and the brain." *Journal of the American Academy of Child and Adolescent Psychiatry 54*, 10, 797.

Young, K. (2011) "Clinical Assessment of Internet-Addicted Clients." In K. Young and C. Nabuco de Abreu (eds) *Internet Addiction: A Handbook and Guide to Evaluation and Treatment.* Hoboken, NJ: John Wiley and Sons.

Young, K. (2015) "The Evolution of Internet Addiction Disorder." In C. Montag and M. Reuter (eds) *Internet Addiction: Neuroscientific Approaches and Therapeutical Interventions.* Basel, Switzerland: Springer.

Young, K. (2016) *The Internet Addiction Test.* Available at http://netaddiction.com/internet-addiction-test, accessed on 2 May 2016.

Yuan, K., Qin, W., Wang, G., Zeng, F. *et al.* (2011) "Microstructure abnormalities in adolescents with internet addiction disorder." *PLoS ONE 6*, 6, e20708.

RESOURCES

Printed material

AAP (American Academy of Pediatrics) (2013) "Children, adolescents and the media: Council on communications and media." *Pediatrics 132*, 5, 58–61.

Baron, N. (2015) *Words Onscreen: The Fate of Reading in a Digital World.* New York, NY: Oxford University Press.

Bauerlein, M. (2011) *The Digital Divide: Arguments for and Against Facebook, Google Texting and the Age of Social Networking.* New York, NY: Penguin.
An interesting collection of essays on both sides of the issues, some a little dated.

Blue, V. (2015) *The Smart Girl's Guide to Privacy: Practical Tips for Staying Safe Online.* San Francisco, CA: No Starch Press.
Truly practical online safety suggestions, not limited to just girls but also useful for boys and adults.

Burley Hofmann, J. (2014) *iRules: What Every Tech-Healthy Family Needs to Know About Selfies, Sexting, Gaming, and Growing Up.* New York, NY: Rodale.
A beautifully written book expanding on "The Contract" of appropriate technology usage originally appearing in the *Huffington Post.* Appropriate technology use is treated as part of a larger responsible lifestyle.

Carr, N. (2011) *What the Internet Is Doing to Our Brains: The Shallows.* New York, NY: W. W. Norton and Company.
Builds the case that electronic reading leads to shallow, superficial thinking.

Gardner, H. and Davis, K. (2014) *The App Generation: How Today's Youth Navigate Identity, Intimacy, and Imagination in a Digital World.* New Haven, CT: Yale University Press.

Greene, R. (2014) *The Explosive Child: A New Approach to Understanding and Parenting Easily Frustrated, Chronically Inflexible Children.* New York, NY: HarperCollins Publishers.

Greenfield, S. (2015) *Mind Change: How Digital Technologies Are Leaving Their Mark on Our Brains.* New York, NY: Random House.

Griffiths, M., Kuss, D., and Demetrovics, Z. (2011) "Social Networking Addiction." In K. Young and C. Nabuco de Abreu (eds) *Internet Addiction: A Handbook and Guide to Evaluation and Treatment.* Hoboken, NJ: John Wiley and Sons.
An authoritative, professional-level book devoted to Internet addiction.

Guernsey, L. (2012) *Screen Time: How Electronic Media—From Baby Videos to Educational Software—Affects Your Young Child.* Philadelphia, PA: Basic Books.

Kutscher, M. (2014) *Kids in the Syndrome Mix of ADHD, LD, Autism Spectrum, Tourette's, Anxiety and More!: The One-Stop Guide for Parents, Teachers, and Other Professionals* (2nd edn). London: Jessica Kingsley Publishers.
Has a chapter on each of the many conditions associated with Internet problems, along with general and specific treatment options.

Kutscher, M. and Moran, M. (2009) *Organizing the Disorganized Child: Simple Strategies to Succeed in School.* New York, NY: HarperCollins Publishers.
Covers setting up an organizational system, as well as reading, writing, and study skills.

Montag, C. and Reuter, M. (eds) (2015) *Internet Addiction: Neuroscientific Approaches and Therapeutical Interventions.* Basel, Switzerland: Springer.
This professional-level book presents a concise multi-authored summary of the state of our scientific understanding of Internet addiction.

Palladino, L. (2015) *Parenting in the Age of Attention Snatchers: A Step-by-Step Guide to Balancing Your Child's Use of Technology.* Boston, MA: Shambhala.
A personalized guide to computer use seen as one aspect of a larger philosophy of life for your children.

Rosen, L. (2012) *iDisorder: Understanding Our Obsession with Technology and Overcoming Its Hold on Us.* New York, NY: Palgrave Macmillan.
An easy-to-comprehend text explaining how digital technology can cause our behavior to mimic many psychiatric conditions, along with simple suggestions to combat the behaviors.

Rosenberg, K. and Feder L. (2014) "An Introduction to Behavioral Addictions." In K. Rosenberg and L. Feder (eds) *Behavioral Addictions: Criteria, Evidence, and Treatment.* London: Elsevier.
Professional-level text covering a range of addictions including Internet, social media, gaming, gambling, sex and more.

Steiner-Adair, C. and Barker, T. (2013) *The Big Disconnect: Protecting Childhood and Family Relationships in the Digital Age.* New York, NY: Harper Collins.
A logical and empathic plea for parents to understand and intervene with screen-time problems.

Thompson, C. (2014) *Smarter than You Think: How Technology is Changing Our Minds for the Better.* New York, NY: Penguin Books.
This text focuses on the positive aspects of technology in ways we may not have considered.

Turkle, S. (2011) *Alone Together: Why We Expect More from Technology and Less from Each Other*. New York, NY: Basic Books.
A well-written book on the psychological effects of technology, written by a leader in the field.

Internet resources
Sites to help control access of content and time

www.commonsensemedia.com offers objective ratings and suggestions for all types of media and all age groups. Ratings include learning potential and appropriate age range. This is an incredibly useful site from a non-profit organization. *Check out this site!*

www.familysafemedia.com offers hardware for limiting access regarding both time and content.

www.getScreen.com aims to allow parents to monitor and set individual controls on all digital devices in their family, including setting time limits on the use of video games and television.

www.TimeTimer.com sells easy-to-set, highly visual timers.

www.livescribe.com describes the livescribe pen. This records the teacher digitally, and plays back whatever was being said at that time when the pen is later touched to the specially coded (but blank appearance) paper. Useful for filling in gaps in notes.

www.KidsBehavioralNeurology.com is the author's website. It contains information about many of the children who are at particular risk of problematic screen time, including those with ADHD or ASD. I will post an updated summary of the American Academy of Pediatrics' media recommendations on my website when they become revised and are published as the "official policy" of the American Academy of Pediatrics.

Sites related to social safety

http://safetynet.aap.org sponsored by the American Academy of Pediatrics, it has fantastic articles and links regarding appropriate use of digital media. *Check out this site!*

www.TeenSafe.com offers parents the opportunity to monitor much of their child's Internet activity.

www.google.com Find the lyrics to any song your child might be listening to by searching this website. Enter into the search bar the word "lyrics" followed by the title of the song or the musical artist's name.

http://mobilemediaguard.com/state_main.html delineates sexting laws in your state.

Sites related to Internet Addiction

http://netaddiction.com is the website of Dr. Kimberly Young, a field leader. It is focused primarily on teens and older. The Internet Addiction Test at http://netaddiction.com/internet-addiction-test is a 20-question validated test that measures where an adult is placed along the spectrum of Internet addiction, from none to mild to moderate to severe.

www.smartrecovery.org strives for scientifically based addiction recovery and has online meetings as well as in-person meetings.

"Internet Addiction: A brief summary of research and practice" is a professional-level article available at www.ncbi.nlm.nih.gov/pmc/articles/PMC3480687.

Disclaimer: Cited materials and websites do not necessarily represent the views or endorsement of the authors.

ABOUT THE AUTHORS

Martin L. Kutscher, MD is a board-certified Pediatric Neurologist specializing in neurobehavioral problems such as ADHD, learning disorders, autism spectrum, anxiety, and tics. He has lectured to parent and professional groups across the US and internationally, and has written four books on the subject: *Kids in the Syndrome Mix of ADHD, LD, Autism Spectrum, Anxiety, Tourette's, and More: The One Stop Guide for Parents, Teachers, and Other Professionals* (2nd edition) (Jessica Kingsley Publishers); *Organizing the Disorganized Child* (with Marcella Moran) (HarperCollins); *ADHD: Living without Brakes* (Jessica Kingsley Publishers); and *The ADHD BOOK: Living Right Now* (Neurology Press). Dr. Kutscher was a member of the Departments of Pediatrics and of Neurology at New York Medical College for more than two decades. His main office is in Rye Brook, New York. Phone: 914-232-1810. Website: www.KidsBehavioralNeurology.com.

Natalie Rosin, CASAMHC is a credentialed substance abuse counselor and mental health specialist. As an individual and family life coach, her areas of expertise are with addiction, mental health disorders, ADHD, and executive function difficulties. Her office is in Rye, New York. She can be reached at 914-967-2438. You can email her at ndrosin@gmail.com. Visit her website at natalierosin.com.

INDEX

abuse, neurological effects of
   digital 40–2, 117
addiction
   biological basis of 99–100
   criteria for 96–7, 125–6
   definition 125
   as disease 106
   healthy enthusiasm vs 95
   psychological basis of 99, 126
   therapy for 106, 127
   see also Internet addiction
ads 27, 87
aggression 42, 57
airbrushing 38, 47, 118
American Academy of Pediatrics
   (AAP) 13, 34, 43, 46–7,
   53–6, 58–60, 62, 64–5, 72,
   83, 110, 115, 119–21
American Psychiatric Association
   (APA) 17, 69–70, 96, 125
anxiety 17, 40, 68, 70, 97, 107, 117
asthma 44, 118
Attention Deficit Hyperactivity
   Disorder (ADHD)
   and ASD 71, 123
   effect of video games 115–16
   extensive use of digital technology
      association with 40
   risks 67–9
   Internet addiction
   prevalence of 100, 123
   as prone to 61, 67–9

prone to need for rapid and
   immediate stimuli 99
spectrum of difficulties in 17
structured play and activities 34
traits making screen time
   appealing 66–7, 122–3
attention system
   daydreaming network 29–30, 114
   and multi-tasking 31–3, 114–15
   need for down-time 33, 115
   screen interference with
      34–5, 115–16
   sensory/emergency network
      29, 67, 114, 122
   stay-on-task network 28–9, 113
   switching between
      networks 30, 114
Autism Spectrum Disorder (ASD)
   association with extensive use
      of digital technology 40
   traits making screen time appealing
   extent of use 71–2, 123
   narrow range of interests/
      behaviors 70
   preference for social media
      73–4, 123–4
   reasons for attraction to
      Internet 70–1, 123
   trouble with social interaction
      and communication
      69–70, 104
   types of use 72–3, 123
   as whole range of disorders 17

137

backache 42, 118
Banger, H. 108
Banger, M. 108
Barker, T. 49, 63, 75, 78, 102, 122
Baron, N. 20, 26, 28
biological basis of addiction 99–100
brain
    and act of reading 23,
        27, 32, 41, 113
    attention to sensory stimuli 80–1
    early childhood
        development 62, 79
    effects of digital technology
        abuse on 40–2, 117
    insula, for switching between
        attention networks
        30, 33, 114–15
    and Internet addiction
        41–2, 99–100, 117
    and "likes" on social media 48
    movement detectors in 27
    plasticity of 40
    and sleep 42
    and video games 33, 41,
        58, 67, 122–3
    voluntary attention centers in 29
    when daydreaming 30, 114
    when faced with hypertext 24–5
Brown, A. 34, 60, 62
Burley Hofmann, J. 43,
    49, 84, 89, 91

Carr, N. 21, 23–4, 30, 32, 112
Cernikova, M. 42
child development, interference
    with 64–5, 122
Christakis, D. 62–3
classroom work, interference
    with 20–2, 111–12
cognitive behavioral therapy
    (CBT) 107, 127
comprehension
    effect of search engines 26
    hypertext diminishing 24–6
    print books better for 26–7, 113

concerns
    historical 14–15
    of parents 11, 16, 111
cyber-bullying 48–9, 118

Dau, W. 108
Davis, K. 33, 37–8, 117
daydreaming
    network 29–30, 114
    positive facets 33
"death by selfie" 44, 118
Demetrovics, Z. 14, 46
depression 17, 39, 68, 96,
    104, 107, 117
dialectic behavioral therapy
    (DBT) 107–8, 127
"digital immigrants" 19
"digital natives" 19, 37
digital technology
    benefits of 12–13, 35–6, 116
    as conduit 19
    as fascinating 102
    meeting psychological needs 102
    rapid explosion of 12, 109–10
    services 12
    terminology 12
    see also Internet; problems;
        screen time
distracting effect
    of hypertext 23, 26, 36, 113
    of reading on digital device 27, 36
Donnerstein, E. 44, 52, 58–9, 120–1
down-time 33, 83, 115
driving injuries 43, 84, 93, 118
Duran, L. 22

Eapen, C. 43
eating habits 43
ereading see reading on-screen

Facebook
    bullying information 49
    privacy 50–1
    as technology service 12, 109
    users/usage 14, 20, 46, 111

family meeting 89–91, 125
family therapy 108, 127
fear 11, 16, 111
Feder, L. 95, 100
Frederick, C. 22
free time
    entertainment in 15
    excessive media use cutting
        into 34, 115
    multi-tasking decreasing 33, 115

Gardner, H. 33, 37–8, 117
Gillespie-Lynch, K. 74
Glatter, R. 43
Greenfield, S. 25, 36, 48,
    50, 57–8, 116
Griffiths, M. 14, 46
Guernsey, L. 64–6, 76–7, 122
Gutenberg printing press 15

happiness 16, 111
hard copy reading
    for engaging in substantial
        work 26, 36
    likelihood of multi-tasking 27
    preference for 27–8, 36, 113
headaches 42, 118
hearing loss 43, 118
Hill, D. 60, 62
Huang, A. 41
hypercholesterolemia 44, 118
hypertension 44, 118
hypertext
    diminishing comprehension 24–5
    as distracting and hard to
        navigate 23–4, 113
    jumps in, as cause of shallow
        reading 25–6

identity 37–8, 117
iGeneration 14, 20, 46, 110–11
imagination 38–9, 117
infants and screen time
    effect of occasional use 65–6
    effect on 3-5-year-olds 64, 122

effect on under-2s 63, 121–2
    interference with child
        development 64–5, 122
    statistics on usage 62, 121
information
    communicating 15
    deep fascination with 70
    evaluation of 86–8
    flow 18
    giving out personal 45,
        50–1, 69, 118
    hiding too much 51–2
    learning from real, live
        sources of 63
    misinterpreting 30
    opportunities through
        Internet 45, 70, 73
    overload 15
    processing 19
    skimming for relevant 26
    surfing for, as less addictive
        103, 126
    visual and sound 15
Internet
    addiction
        addictive activities 103, 126
        addictive nature of digital
            media 100–2
        ADHD children at risk
            of 61, 67–9, 123
        and ASD children 70–1, 123
        biological basis of 99–100
        and the brain 41–2,
            99–100, 117
        criteria for 96–8, 125–6
        definition 16
        personal traits associated
            with 104
        prevalence of 100
        psychological basis of 99, 126
        spectrum of problem
            severity 95, 98, 100
        treating 105–8, 127
        types of 98
        websites related to 135

Internet *cont.*
 affecting "free-time"
  entertainment 15
 affecting social interaction
  15, 45–7
 benefits of 12–13
 invasive ads 27
 neurological effects of abuse 117
 no such thing as privacy on 50–1
 psychological effects of 117
 as solution for information
  overload 15
 teenage exposure to sexual
  content in US 54
 terminology 12
 see also digital technology;
  problems; screen time
intimacy 38, 117
introspection 33
involuntary attention 29–30, 80, 114

Jordan, A. 44, 52, 58–9, 120–1

Kennedy Krieger Institute 43
Kuo, M. 72–3
Kuss, D. 14, 46
Kutscher, M. 70, 85, 136

learning effects
 for under 2s 63, 121–2
 advantages of digital 35–6, 116
 of daydreaming 30, 114
 interference with classroom
  work 20–2, 84, 111–12
 of music 31–2, 84
 perceptions of 19–20
 on-screen reading 23–8, 112–13
 summary of digital vs print 36–7
 taking notes on laptop 22–3, 112
Lei, H. 41
Levitin, D. 28, 30
"likes" 38, 48, 117–18
limiting use of digital
 technology *see* parents
Lin, F. 41
Lin, X. 100

Loh, K. 19, 25, 27, 31, 41, 113
Lunsky, Y. 73

Macmullin, J. 73
Massively Multiplayer Online
 Role Playing Games
 (MMORPG) 103, 126
Mazurek, M. 73
Moran, M. 85, 136
motivational interviewing 106
Mueller, P. 22
multi-switching 31–2, 80,
 82, 114–15, 125
multi-tasking
 avoiding 82, 93
 and brain 41
 of digital natives 19
 myth of 31–3, 114–15
 while reading digitally 27, 36
musculoskeletal pain 42, 118
music
 hearing loss due to loud 43
 multi-tasking with 31–2
 sexual content 54, 58, 118–20
 violence exposure 56, 58, 119–20
 while doing homework 84, 94

navigation and orientation
 difficulties 24–5, 123
neurological effects of digital
 abuse 27, 40–2, 113, 117
note-taking 22–3, 112

obesity 59, 120, 211111
on-screen reading *see*
 reading on-screen
Oppenheimer, D. 22

Palladino, L. 28, 35, 80–1
parents
 allowing TVs in child's
  room 77, 101
 co-viewing 62, 72, 76
 concerns of 11, 16, 111
 duties 59–60
 heavy media use of 59, 76–7, 121

interaction with children
60, 64–6, 122
media rules 13, 47, 110, 118
methods of setting limits
help develop voluntary attention
control 80–2, 124–5
helpful websites 134–5
rule equality 85
set explicit time rules in
advance 82–5
teach information
evaluation 86–8
use technology to limit
technology 79–80, 124
monitoring 45, 56
role in setting limits 16, 111
as role model
replacement by media 56, 119
type of 75–8, 124
setting controls 51–2, 124, 134
setting up rules
family meeting 89–91, 125
screen time agreement 91–4
teaching of conflict resolution 49
pen and paper, advantages
of using 22–3, 112
physical effects of digital
technology use 42–4, 118
plasticity of brain 40
play
structured 34, 60, 82, 115–16
unstructured 34, 60, 64–5,
115–16, 122
pornography see sexual content
Porter, A. 20, 111
pride 16, 111
privacy 50–1, 79, 92
problematic screen time
17, 97–8, 100
problems
associated with specific populations
children with ADHD
66–9, 122–3
children with ASD
69–74, 123–4
dangers and opportunities 61

infants 62–6, 121–2
with content of digital technology
dangers and opportunities 45
recommendations regarding
58–60, 120–1
sexual 52–5, 118–19
social media 46–52, 118
and substance use 58, 120
violent 55–8, 119–20
of Internet addiction
addictiveness of digital
media 100–3, 126
becoming addicted
99–100, 126
nature of addiction 96–8, 125–6
personal traits associated
with 104
prevalence of 100
spectrum of problem
severity 95, 98, 100
treating 105–8, 127, 135
spectrum of severity 16–17
with use of digital technology
association with psychological
conditions 39–40, 117
cutting into play time
34, 115–16
diminishing benefits of
down-time 33, 115
interference with classroom
work 20–2, 111–12
interfering with developing
voluntary attention
34–5, 116
neurological effects of
abuse 40–2, 117
note-taking 22–3, 112
physical effects 42–4, 118
psychological/learning effects
of 19–28, 36–9, 111–17
on-screen reading
23–8, 112–13
Products Safety Project 44
psychological basis of addiction 99
psychological conditions,
association with 39–40, 117

psychological effects 19–20, 37–9, 117
psychological needs, digital technology meeting 102
psychosis 17

re-invention 47, 118
reading
    and families with heavy media use 65
    as multi-sensory experience 23
    neurological connections for deep 27, 40, 113
    skills needed in 22
reading on-screen
    benefits of 35–6, 116
    distracting effect 27, 36
    lacking tactile experience 23, 113
    navigation and orientation difficulties 24–5, 123
    preference for hard-copy reading 27–8, 36, 113
    shallow 19, 25–7, 113
ready access 101
repetitive movement thumb injury 43, 118
Rideout, V. 14
Rosen, L. 12–14, 20–1, 32, 46, 97, 109–12
Rosenberg, K. 95, 100

Salie, F. 44
Science Daily 43
screen time
    agreement
        family meeting 89–91, 125
        negotiable privileges 93–4
        non-negotiable rules 92–3
    balancing
        achieving 79–88, 124–5
        importance of 75–9, 124
    children with ADHD 66–9, 122–3
    children with ASD 69–74, 123–4
    components of 12, 109

extent of usage 13–14, 110
    of infants
        for under 2s 63, 121–2
        for 3-5 year olds 64, 122
        background television 64–5, 122
        occasional use 65–6
        statistics on usage 62, 121
    interference
        with developing voluntary attention 34–5, 116
        unstructured play, structured play, and other activities 34, 60, 115–16
    need for down-time 33, 83, 115
    spectrum of problem severity 16–17, 95, 100
    see also digital technology; Internet; problems
search engines 26–7, 86
selfies 44, 47, 118
sensory/emergency network 29–30, 67, 114, 122
setting limits/rules see parents
sexting 49–50, 118
sexual content
    effects on sexuality 52–3
    exposure to
        relationship with adolescent sexual behavior 54–5
        teenage, in US 53
    recommendations regarding 58–60, 120–1
sexuality
    effects of sexual content on 52–3, 118–19
    relationship with exposure to sexual content 54–5
    teenage, in US 53
Shifrin, D. 60, 62
sleep, effects on 42, 73, 84, 118
Smahel, D. 42
social interaction 15, 57, 60, 69, 120

social media
  appeal of
    addictive "likes" 48
    re-invention/airbrushing
      of life 47
  benefits of 52, 61
  cyber-bullying 48–9
  extent of use 46–7
  information
    giving out too much 45,
      50–1, 69, 118
    hiding too much 51–2
  and people with ASD 74
  risks to people on autism
    spectrum 61
  sexting 49–50
special needs students 36–7, 116
spectrum of problem severity
  16–17, 95, 98, 100
stay-on-task network 28–30, 113
Steiner-Adair, C. 49, 63,
  75, 78, 102, 122
Strasburger, V. 44, 52, 58–9, 120–1
substance use 58, 120
Suris, J.C. 42

tactile experience 23, 113
televisions
  under-2s viewing 62, 121–2
  almost constant use of,
    in families 77
  ASD adolescent viewing
    71–2, 123
  background, interference
    with child development
    31, 62, 64–5, 122
  in children's rooms 13, 43,
    46, 55–6, 59, 73, 77, 83,
    101, 110, 119–20
  exposure to sexual content
    54–5, 58, 118–19
  injuries from falling 44, 118
  and language delay 63, 65, 122
  and multi-tasking 32
  physical effects associated
    with heavy use of 44
  user controls 79

  violence on 56, 58, 119
Thompson, C. 20, 86, 112
thumb injury 43, 118
treating Internet addiction
  helpful websites 135
  impossibility of total
    abstinence 105–6, 127
  prevention as best remedy
    105, 127
  therapist interventions 106–8, 127

University of Illinois Library 86–7

"Vault apps" 51
video games
  addiction to 41, 99–100
  and ADHD 66–9, 122–3
  and ASD 71–3
  engaging attention 27, 30, 41, 114
  multi-switching 80
  multi-tasking with 27, 32–3, 41
  need for down-time 33
  parental help with difficulties
    regarding 80–1
  reinforcing negative traits
    34, 115–16
  and sensory detectors 29
  violent, leading to violent
    behavior 57–8, 119–20
violent content
  exposure to, increasing risk of
    violent behavior 55–6, 119
  recommendations regarding
    58–60, 120–1
  of video games, leading to violent
    behaviour 57–8, 119–20
voluntary attention
  children with ADHD 122
  definition 34
  helping child develop control
    of 80–2, 124–5
  interference with developing
    34–5, 116
  stay-on-task network as 29, 113
  working with involuntary
    attention 30

walking injuries 43, 118
websites
  children with ASD
    computer time spent by 71
    type visited by 73
  evaluation of 86–8
  to help control access of
    content and time 134
  related to Internet addiction 135
  related to social safety 134

Weinstrup, C. 73
Weiss, J. 73
Weiss, M. 68, 100, 108
White, T. 17
Wright, M. 42

young children *see* infants
  and screen time
Young, K. 96, 98, 100, 106
Yuan, K. 42, 117